Daddy's Eyes

POWER HOUSE

Daddy's Eyes

Learning to See through Blinded Eyes

Inspiring Stories of Faith, Hope, and Love

Rachel Houston

Cover and interior book design by Michelle Everett for POWER HOUSE, © 2023 Power House Studios, LLC.

Published by: **Power House**

An imprint of Power House Studios LLC.

thepowerhousestudio.com

PO Box 101678

Cape Coral FL 33910

Home of *The Power House Blueprint* ™ Concierge Publishing System

Dedication

I dedicate this book to you, Dad. You are the inspiration for this book, sharing your life's accounts from your unique perspective. It is entertaining but also gives us great insight into your upbringing and how you used that training to raise four daughters. I am so thankful for the disciplined life you patterned in front of my sisters and me. You have followed the Lord to the best of your ability and worked to impart those Godly values and morals to us. I am so grateful for your guidance and example. Thank you, Dad, for living your life to the full and by demonstrating by your actions how to truly follow the Lord. I will strive to follow the Lord with the zeal you instilled in me.

Acknowledgments

I want to acknowledge my sisters who experienced the teaching and upbringing of our dad along with me. Each can shed light on various aspects of what we embarked upon growing up on the Welch farm. Each one can explain different life lessons we learned from Dad. Thank you, Lord, that we didn't destroy one another no matter how much we disagreed or fought.

To my God-given husband Jason, who has stood beside me through all ups and downs in our journey in life together. Thank you for loving this hardheaded Missouri girl, no matter what. I am blessed to walk along with you through this ministry journey. You always encourage me, challenge me and share your wisdom on so many things. You make it easy to submit to your leadership as the head of our household. I trust you with my whole life.

To my two children, Alex and Aaron, who have challenged me to be a better mother and leader. You two continually bring me joy by loving the Lord and sharing the light of the Word of God with all you come in contact with. I am beyond blessed to be your mother.

To my dearest friend, Debra (who I like to call my spiritual momma), you always speak life and encouragement into me. You are a solid woman of faith who heeds the prompting of the Holy Spirit. I admire how you walk in love, live out your life in love, and shine forth the love of God to all in your midst. You have often been a sounding board and an ear to listen to my ramblings.

To my guide, protector, counselor, vision giver, promise keeper Lord. I cannot make it in this world without Holy Spirit. He leads me into all truth. He points me to Jesus—the author and finisher of my faith. He elevates the goodness of God. May I always follow, hear, and do what you prompt in my heart.

Preface

Have you ever wondered why you grew up as you did? Why were you living where you were living? Why is it that you have the siblings that you do? Or why are you an only child?

I am sure that each one reading this can relate to the multiple whys that come as we are growing up or even as we have become an adult concerning our childhood. Sitting around asking these questions to oneself can bring up so many emotions and feelings that we often do not want to stir up or even talk about. Also, each of us can recant a different story of how we were raised. We can dive into the pains and joys that flood our minds when we discuss our childhood. Not one of us has the same story. Not even each of us raised in the same household can tell the exact same stories and feelings within those stories.

We can all share such vivid details of memories of long ago and allow others a sneak peek into our life stories. This is one of those moments where you can get a glimpse into the lives of a father and his daughter—how what he learned and what he was taught affected how she learned and was taught. Generation to generation is seen in these stories, all revealing lives who grew in faith, hope, and love. This is a powerful reminder that the lineage and legacy passed down can inspire others to embrace their story and see it differently, perhaps with gratitude and growth replacing grief and sorrows.

I have always wondered about my childhood and life in general. It wasn't until after my mother transitioned to her eternal home in April 2019 that I honed in on my upbringing even more than ever before. I began to focus on the only parent left, my dad, who for my whole life has been legally blind. I always was fascinated by how he conducted his daily routines and never considered himself to have a disability. While pondering his many amazing feats, the Lord dropped in my spirit to write this book about him. This book introduces you to my dad, Wilbur Leroy Welch. Through this book, I hope to inspire others with just a glimpse of his ordinary yet extraordinary life and how he saw things—things that many fully-sighted people never see.

You will gain insight into life from the perspective of a person who may have lost his eyesight but truly gained so much by developing his other senses. Not only did he adapt and learn to fully live, but he taught me to do the same, not to rely on only one sense but how to develop all my senses. I can only speak for myself, but I know I am a better-developed person because of who my father is. As I have grown in the knowledge of the Lord, I can clearly see how God has used that training to develop me uniquely for His Kingdom.

As he and I share the journey in the pages ahead, offering glimpses into the life of my Dad, Leroy Welch, and some glimpses into my life, I pray that you are gripped by what is said. I pray that you are moved by the power of God and inspired by faith, hope, and love. I pray that you will be able to see like never before that the creator God has positioned you for greatness. He has called you for such a time as this. No matter what you have been through or are going through, He can take that and create the most beautiful masterpiece.

I am honored to share the marvelous ways Dad learned to see through blinded eyes and how he has grabbed hold of what he was created for through his 87 years of life (and counting). He was created to glorify and magnify the name of the Lord. He was created to raise his daughters to become women that raise their children in the love and admonition of the Lord.

No matter what you have seen thus far, you have an open invitation to view your own lives through God's empowering Grace.

I invite you to join me now in these most enduring and endearing stories of life, where we discover that just like Dad, we can choose our perspective...

We can learn to see through blinded eyes.

Contents

Chapter One
Sunrise

The year was 1936. The world was deep in the heart of the great depression. Businesses had gone under, and multiple lives were distressed by the stock market crash and the devastation of the losses of houses, farms, and land. The grip of starvation had hit hard during this time-frame. President Franklin D. Roosevelt was at the end of his first term and won by a landslide in the election of 1936 to begin his second term. St. Louis, Missouri, recorded having a "relentless, withering heat wave in 1936"[1] that cost hundreds of lives. Severe drought wreaked havoc on huge sections of the Midwest and plains of nineteen states, producing dust storms that created the now well-known term for the area, the Dust Bowl of the American Midwest.

The average cost of a new home was $3,925.00. The cost of a gallon of gas was ten cents. A Studebaker Car was $665.00. The average wages for the year were around $1700.00.[2] In 1936, the most famous person in America was probably Jesse Owens (famous track and field athlete). The price of the Monopoly Board game was $1.98. The Phantom made his debut in newspaper comic strips. And the Great Sphinx of Giza (once buried up to its shoulders in sand) was being completely excavated that year.[3]

Despite all the turmoil in the world during that season, there were hubs of joy. One was in the Welch household. Early on in that year, Rachel (Lockard) Welch delivered her first son into this world. His sunrise was on Thursday, January 30, 1936. The joy of his arrival was overwhelming as this bright blue-eyed little child looked up at his parents. The economy and world events took a pause as this family embraced the bundle of life that burst on the scene on that day. This family was no longer a family of three but of four. His older sister Vonetta was so excited to have someone besides her mom and dad to talk to. It was as if she had gained her own real life baby doll to love and care for. Vonetta was seven years old when her baby brother entered this world. Wilbur Leroy Welch came upon the scene that glorious day, and life would never be the same again. Rachel and her husband Ralph Welch lived at a place called Laceyville (west of Adrian, Missouri, about five miles off of 18 Highway) when little Leroy was delivered.

Leroy grew up in what seemed like the manner that every other child did during those times. He was often found following alongside his father, Ralph, and doing what he said to do. Leroy learned many things from his dad before even reaching school age. He learned to get up when told and help his mom when she asked him to complete a chore or a task. Leroy learned to listen to his big sister Vonetta when she asked him to do something—she kept him in line. He learned to feed and take care of the animals. He learned to help work on the farm equipment by handing his dad his tools. Leroy learned the importance of work and how that family was important. He learned that helping out one another was just something you did. He learned to help plant crops, pick vegetables, and tend to the garden.

Leroy was a young fella that enjoyed being outside as much as possible. Like others who grew up on farms and worked alongside their families, he learned most everything needed to keep the farm going and make ends meet. He also learned to just do whatever was asked of him by his parents. Despite being like many other children during that period, a stark difference between Leroy and other children his age set him apart for life. There was a development in Leroy that cannot be pinned down to where it came from or how he obtained it.

Leroy grew up with a visual disability and was legally blind from an early age. In addition to his vision difficulties, all of his siblings also developed visual disabilities that varied in degrees from one to the other. All seven children—two boys and five girls—were raised in the 1940s. All surviving children, six of them, developed visual disabilities, each one with a different diagnosed eye condition resulting in legal blindness.

Between Leroy's birth and school age, the family moved to another area just northwest of Butler, Missouri, closer to my grandmother's family on the Lockard homestead. It was not unusual for the family to move around from place to place since they rented the houses and the farmland from others.

After a long wait and a bit of growing up, the year finally arrived for Leroy to attend school. He had to wait almost seven years to start because his birthday was in January. He felt a little behind already because he could not start like some of his peers did the year earlier. He was so excited to start school and finally learn all these wonderful things his older sister had spoken of.

Leroy was ready to discover how to do arithmetic and hear all the stories from history. He wanted to learn all the great stuff he had heard that school would give him. He wanted to learn to read so he could read all the time. He also wanted a small break from all the work he had to do on the farm because he was not in school yet.

Having introduced you to Leroy through his arrival in the family, from here on out in the text, I refer to Leroy as "my dad" or "Dad." To avoid confusion, I want to establish that in the direct quotes from my father (which will be either in quotation marks or indented block quotations) the name Dad refers to his father (Ralph Welch) and the name Mom refers to his mother (Rachel Lockard Welch). We continue our story now with one of my dad's favorite memories of starting school and the new experiences that opened up to him:

Learning to See Through Blinded Eyes

The schoolhouse was about one mile away from the farmhouse they lived in. So, my dad (Leroy) set out to walk on his first trip to school with his older sister, Vonetta, walking with him. He arrived at the schoolhouse to start his learning journey. The name of the schoolhouse was Prairie Rose, which according to my dad, was "located five miles north of Butler, then one and three quarters west and then about half a mile north (out in the middle of nowhere)." He was super excited to begin working on all those "lessons" the teacher had to give him.

It was an extremely cold winter that year, and Vonetta had to keep beating on me to get me to stay awake as we walked home from school. I would take a few steps, and then I felt her beat on my back and shoulders, telling me to stay awake. It was bitter cold outside, and I was so tired. That walk home seemed like forever, but I will never forget her beating on me. Vonetta was not about to let me fall asleep or get hurt on the way home because she would have been in big trouble for sure. She was always helping me out. Don't know why she didn't pick me up and carry me, but she didn't. We made it back home safely, thank the Lord. I also remember doing everything I could to go to bed early that day.

During the beginning part of his first year of school, my dad became extremely sick with scarlet fever:

Daddy's Eyes

I was really sick, and the whole house had to be quarantined. All of us were sick in some way. I do not recall if all of us had the same sickness; I just remember how awful it was and that we were all sick. There was a neighbor that would go get us groceries and bring all of it to the door since none of us could get out and get anything. They would knock on the door and then leave. Then Mom [Rachel] or Vonetta would open the door, get it all, and bring it in the house. I had a horrible fever and cough and was so weak during that time. I did not really feel like eating much at all. Mom had to force me to even eat a little, which you know is a big deal since you know I really love to eat. I did not know if I was going to make it or not. It seemed like it lasted for weeks, but I cannot remember how long it was. It was a horrible time in my life. I am so thankful that I recovered from that horrible sickness.

Although that was a challenge for the whole family, a fond memory that my dad recalls from that first school year was of his own father working as a mail carrier:

I recall Dad [Ralph] was working as a mail carrier. He would ride a horse (Lady) and go pick up mail over at Passaic (where the mail came through by train) and carry mail to little stores and family dwellings. I do not know how many of them there

were, but I remember a few of them specifically because Dad would talk about some of them. He would
even deliver to various little towns and had to ride
the horse to each little place of dwelling and town.
About every six or seven miles, there was a little town
or store of some sort. Back then, it took almost the
whole day for you to travel to the nearest town and
back. Most people would go to town to get their groceries and mail and such, and then [they] got back
home all in that day. It seemed Dad had about eight
or nine little towns, mostly west and south of Passaic, that he would deliver mail to. Dad stayed terribly
busy as a mail carrier. I often wanted to get up on
Lady and ride around like Dad did.

Besides having to wait to start school and shortly after
starting school getting extremely sick, my dad faced much
turmoil in his early school years. In the middle of his second
year of school, the Welch family ended up having to move
from rural Butler, Missouri, to Florence, Colorado. This occurred shortly after his younger sister Sarah (who was around
three at the time) died and was buried. My dad recalls,

We decided to move out to Florence because of
Dad. Here is the story. His number was called [in the
military draft], and so he went to Kansas so they could
get him checked out and ready for the war. They told
him to get all of his things squared away, sell what he

needed to, and then come back for medical testing. So, Dad came back home. We sold the trailer he had built and many other things. Jewell [Leroy's brother] and I helped them load up all the hay so we could get that sold. They sold all the machinery quickly when Dad got back because they told him he had to get everything done so fast since he was being moved out for the war. All we had left was a Dodge 2-ton truck that had a pitched roof on the back of it that Dad had built on to keep what little furniture we had dry.

We decided to take some of the wagons and the horses over to Grandpa Alonzo's instead of selling them. That way, Grandpa could use them on the farm. We had no idea what was in store for our family. But since they told Dad that he had to get rid of everything because he was going into the military, we had to do what we had to do. [Author's note: Grandpa Alonzo was my dad's maternal grandfather, the father of my grandmother, who was also named Rachel.]

Dad had to go back to Kansas (where the base was) shortly after his first visit to have his medical testing. He went to do the medical testing, and then they told him that he had something wrong with his lungs, so he could not go to war! They told him that with whatever was going on in his lungs, he should consider moving to an area like Colorado. Dad came home so mad he could have spit nails and built a fence. It was horrible that we had sold most everything and even told the people we rented from we were not going to be there. Dad and Mom had some serious decisions to make. Since we had lots of family in Colorado and had already sold most everything, we headed to Colorado. Junior [Ralph's brother] was working at a mine there in Colorado near Florence, and there was an opening there. So, we headed there after burying Sarah.

Dad-isms and replies...

"Dad, how do you feel?" I ask.
"With my hands, of course," he replies.

Chapter Two
School Days

For a brief time after the Welch family first arrived in Colorado, my dad and his siblings could not go to school because they lived near the mine and were not in town. This situation was not ideal for the Welch family, so Ralph and Rachel decided to locate a house in town so the kids could go to school. My dad remembers it this way:

> We found a house in town by the Arkansas River and lived there for a little over a year. We would help Dad pick apples, raspberries, and strawberries from a German farmer on his ranch. Now Uncle Nobel [Ralph's brother] was working at a big ranch, so Dad got on there to work for a season. The name of the ranch was something like Hillside Ranch, I think.

While living in Colorado, my dad was in the second grade, and he recalled, "I went to school, and I could not see the blackboard from the seats. I could not even make out the numbers on the board to write in my tablet. I would have to walk up the blackboard and try to focus on what was up there. I could make stuff out better by getting up close." He went home and told his parents he was having trouble seeing the lessons at school. He was eventually taken to a German eye doctor in Pueblo, Colorado. The optometrist thoroughly examined his eyes and vision and diagnosed him with retina deterioration. My dad was laughing so hard when he was telling this story; you can tell it must have been a sight to see:

> The doctor said we could try some vitamin and mineral stuff, but that was about all they could do for me. I do not recall if they checked us all out that day or not. Let me tell you about that day we went to the eye doctor. After the appointment, I could barely see a thing with all that crud they put in my eyes, but I remember what was going on because I could hear it clearly.
>
> Later on, Mom filled me in with the details of what was really going on: There was a bus coming into the town [Pueblo], and a woman was hanging out of the window hollering at Mom and Dad extremely loud. She kept trying to get their attention as the bus was coming in. It was Grandma Bishop [Ralph's mother], who had come to town on the bus and was trying to wave Mom and Dad down so she could ride back home to Florence with them. I heard someone hollering but couldn't quite make it out, and I definitely couldn't see anything after that exam.

Learning to See Through Blinded Eyes

Mom told me it was Grandma Bishop caterwauling and hanging out the window from the bus. You could hear in the tone of Mom's voice that she was not too happy about all the ruckus that Grandma Bishop had caused. Boy, was that a day to remember!

Despite all the vitamins and minerals the doctor suggested, my dad's eyes continued to deteriorate, so he still had to get right up in front of the blackboard while at school in Colorado. Staying back in his seat like the others was not an option if he wanted to complete his lessons.

Dad stated that he could see better when he was right close to smaller things like words or numbers. He seemed to do alright with bigger things like people's outlines and trees and such. Even with that, Dad still could not fully identify the details of things.

While in Colorado, he continued to do his best at school by adjusting his position of learning. No additional tools or adaptive equipment were available for him at that time in school. He had to learn to work with what he could do and rely on the teachers and himself to figure out how to complete his lessons. Dad told me it was difficult and different initially, but he adjusted to it. Sadly, Dad said that as soon as he adjusted to the new school and began to find his groove there, they had to move again.

After working with his brother Noble on the ranch for a season, my Grandpa Ralph switched to work with his brother Junior at the mine there near Florence. My dad said it wasn't long after my grandpa began working at the mine that the family had to decide where to live again.

While Dad was working for the mine, he wasn't down in the mine like a lot of them were. He was more on the outside, but he ended up having another medical test run by the mining company. They said Dad could not work there anymore because of what they found on the test. The mining company suggested he move down to someplace like Arizona because his lungs did not look good. Dad did not want to move down there, so Mom and Dad decided to just go back to Missouri since Mom's family was there. Again, Dad was not happy, to say the least, but what was he going to do? So, we started back towards Missouri in '45.

On our way back to Missouri, we had to stop at Uncle Ebert and Aunt Phoebe's because of Mom. See, she had a miscarriage on the way back, and Dad had to stop and pull over by the side of the road. Dad dug a hole and buried the fetus by a cedar tree.

Vonetta had to drive the chevy car back since Mom was unable to drive. She was about 15 or 16 because I was in the 3rd grade at that time. So, we stopped at Uncle Ebert and Aunt Phoebe's since Mom had to rest and was still bleeding. They were living in Coldwater, Kansas, at the time. So, I guess the fetus is somewhere in Kansas between Coldwater and the

Colorado border. We stayed there for a little bit until Mom stopped bleeding and was strong enough to ride to Missouri.

We moved back here to Missouri in 1945 because Nancy Joanne was born in '46. When we got back, we stayed with Aunt Canny [Alonzo's sister-in-law] for just a little while. Then we lived on the road back from the farm. It was a two-story house that joined the backside of Grandpa Alonzo's farm. Nancy Joanne was born there in that house. The man we were renting from there ended up cheating Mom and Dad out of a lot of money. We did not want to deal with him anymore, so we decided to move to the Case place over near Johnstown.

My dad told me that after moving back from Colorado and moving over to the place closer to Johnstown that he was in the 4th grade. He recalled a couple of stories from his school days when he was over at Johnstown:

I remember when us kids lived on the hill over on the Case place. Of course, we had to walk to school. In order to get to the school, first, we had to walk down the hill about a quarter of a mile to cross over the Deep Water creek, a spot where the two creeks would meet, to get to the Johnstown schoolhouse.

There was a man by the name of Mr. Whitman who would run his John Deer Tractor every morning. If he could not get his tractor to run, he would run his motor. He had a one-cylinder gas-powered motor that we called Putt-Putt because of the sound it made. There were mornings that he would have Putt-Putt running down toward the bottom of the hill, especially when it was extremely foggy. The fog would be so thick we could not really see the road, but we could hear Putt-Putt and follow that sound across the creeks.

From there, we headed north past the Johnstown Church of Christ and then on over to the Johnstown schoolhouse. There were some days we would follow the sound of that tractor when he had it running, and then we knew we were close to the church. Once we arrived at the church, we could continue farther north to the schoolhouse.

It was a big two-story school and had an upstairs in it with a couple of small-like classes. The majority of the classes were downstairs, though. They called it a one-room schoolhouse; at least, that is what it was when we left there. They had both a coal stove and a wood-burning stove in there that kept the downstairs pretty warm. I cannot remember the exact number of kids that attended there, but if I had to take a guess, I would say around 20 or so.

I do remember our teacher. Her name was Mrs. Stevens. Mrs. Stevens had this car, which I cannot remember what kind it was, but it had running boards on the side of it. There were times if we timed it right, we could catch a ride on the running boards or the luggage rack on the back of the car or the fender on the way up north to the school. Sometimes we could ride on her running boards for a quarter mile to a half a mile since the school was just north of Johnstown.

The school was a good quarter mile from the main part of town where the store, post office, and telephone office with the switchboards were located. There was even an old-fashioned blacksmith shop there as well.

I spent the majority of my school years there at the Johnstown School. I was in high school before we ever left there and went to Butler. It was right before I left Johnstown that they put in a bus route. I have some fond memories of that school. I hate that it burnt down not long after we left and is no longer there.

All throughout my school days, I had to go up to the blackboard to see the words. The older I got, the bigger the words had to be for me to see them. The numbers on the blackboard had to be lined up just right for me to do my arithmetic. If I had to complete that work at home, I would imagine the blackboard and the numbers on the blackboard and picture myself doing the arithmetic. Then, I would tell Mom the answers, and she would help me write them down in the correct spots. On occasion, Vonetta would write it for me. If I did not have help with my writing, I would have the spacing mixed up sometimes since it was so small.

Mom had to read the books to us, so we could hear our lessons, and then we would tell our teacher the answers when we got to school the next day. Boy, I had to remember it all. For most of the lessons, I had to memorize what Mom had read to us the night before. Now, Mom would read at least two lessons, sometimes three. She did not have to help Vonetta as much as she did Wilma, Jewell, and me. Now Wilma and I were in the same grade, so our lessons were the same, and that helped Mom out. Then she would have to read Jewell's. He was the year or next behind Wilma and me. Mom loved to read and was amazing at reading. There were times she would have to read it a couple of times as we were trying to remember all the information for our lessons. I know I tried to memorize as many details as possible. I tried to tie the lesson to a picture film, and that seemed to help me recite it back the next day.

Mom always was patient with us kids and wanted us to get the lesson right. She would work so hard to get all that done as well as everything else she had to do. I remember times when Mom was cooking, holding one of the kids on her hip, and reading our lessons all at the same time. She was an amazing mother, for sure. I never recall Mom ever complaining about having to do extra with us kids. She just did what she did with grace and pleasure. She was the best Mom a person could ever have.

I also never recall Dad complaining about it either. If they ever said anything about having six kids with eye issues, they never relayed it to where I could hear it. They loved us like parents should and kept us busy training us how to do what needed to be done on the farm. We worked as a family to get things accomplished and were not given any time for excuses because things had to be done regardless. We just all worked together and figured out a way to complete the task, and we got it done.

Throughout my school years, there were some boys that did not really know us. We would come in contact with them, and they would try to get one over on us since we were "the blind kids." But Jewell and I could whup up on them pretty quickly. After that, they didn't seem to try to bother us. The other kids at the school were always so nice and helpful. We were blessed to be around lots of people who were more willing to help us blind kids than take advantage of us. Lots of us grew up together and became close friends. More times than not, they treated us so kindly and friendly and were always so helpful.

My favorite subject in school was history. I loved hearing about the battles and where they took place. I enjoyed hearing about the different important historic people and what they did, and how they invented things. I would picture what they looked like. I would picture the cities and what the battles looked like. I could imagine what was taking place as I was listening to the lessons being read by Mom.

I guess you could say I get my love for reading from Mom. When I hear the books being read, I can picture the whole thing in my mind, and it is like a movie playing. If there are not lots of descriptions, I get to make up my own interpretation of what is being read.

I create what I think the characters looked like, how they were dressed, and their builds. I see all these things in my mind and get lost in the book and the story as I listen. I really pay attention to what is being said and then let my imagination run wild. Reading takes me to all kinds of wonderful places that I couldn't go to or visit any other way.

I do the same thing when I read the Bible. I picture what each person looks like and how the cities were. It is like I am there when I hear it being read.

After living near Johnstown for a good while, my dad and the rest of his family moved over to the Lockard family farm. He finished his high school years at Butler High School and graduated there. Dad and my aunts and uncle would ride the bus from the end of our road into Butler, Missouri, to attend the school, which was a distance of eight miles.

A fun fact to interject is that the Lockard family farm still exists; the farm has been in our family for well over 100 years, and although he is mostly retired from farm work, my dad still lives on this farm.

While at Butler High School, my dad recalls wanting to join the school choir:

> That choir teacher said I could not be in the choir because I could not see the music to read it. All I had to do was hear the music, and I would have gotten it. Wilma and two other girls had a trio and went around the school all the time, singing away. They sounded so amazing together. I really wanted to be in the choir—because, you know, I love to sing, especially for the Lord.

Shortly after moving back to Missouri, they needed to find another eye doctor, one that was closer to them. They went to an eye doctor in Nevada, Missouri, but that doctor said he could do nothing to help. He sent them to a special eye doctor in Kansas City. That doctor said he did not have retina deterioration but something called Retinitis Pigmentosa. My dad recalls,

> He put me on a different vitamin and mineral program, but it did not help at all. I was continuing to lose my sight. He said it was that RT/RP, but it was not. We did not continue to use him. After that,

Daddy's Eyes

I went to other eye doctors. The other eye doctors I seen went back to the original diagnosis of deterioration of the retina. Each eye doctor visit was about the same report. "Your eyes are worse than the last time and will continue to deteriorate until you will not see anything at all." I have watched my eyes get worse for sure but have fought to keep my memories of what others and things looked like in my mind.

When asked about the doctors that recommended the vitamins and what else he tried that could have possibly helped him see better, he replied,

You know, I tried the vitamin and mineral program. I tried wearing special glasses. But other than that, they did not do much. It was then they decided to try to send me to the School of the Blind to see if that would work. I went to the School of the Blind in St. Louis when I was twelve and thirteen [1948,1949]. Vonetta was there with me as well, but only for a year. She had the best eyesight of us all and learned to use a magnifier quite well. Mom and Dad did not send any of the rest of the kids. I can remember the address of the school to this day. It was 3815 Magnolia, one block west of Grand across from Tyre Park. While there, they tried to get me to use the magnifying stuff. I could not stand the magnifier because I would get deathly sick. I would get extreme motion sickness, and I felt like a duck who had been drinking and trying to walk straight on one leg. Won't use those things. NO. NO. NO. They said I had enough sight (at the time) to read large print, so I did not learn much Braille. I learned all my numbers and the basics of reading Braille but was not fully able to read it.

After I returned home from the School of the Blind, my eyes began to get even worse. Since they felt I did not need to learn Braille, I had to figure out how to make it through school without being able to read the school's books. Sometimes I wish I would have learned more Braille, but the Lord has helped me get through each and every day well.

Dad-isms and reading...

Dad picked up a magazine, and I asked, "Dad are you fixing to read that?" His reply was priceless. "My backside is going to get up close and personal with every article in here" (as he carried it with him to the outhouse).

Dad-isms and replies...

"Dad, I better hop off the phone for now."

"Okay, well, be careful; we don't want any broken bones," snickering as he says it.

Chapter Three
Conversations with Dad

There were so many questions I asked my dad as I was preparing for this book. When we take the time to have conversations, many things can be learned, and priceless treasures can be discovered. During those conversations, countless precious stories were recorded that could not be included in this book as I endeavored to apply reasonable limits on page count and my project completion time. So, perhaps there will be another book one day for those! But in this chapter, I want to share a few special highlights from those many conversations with Dad:

"Dad, if you didn't learn Braille at the School of the Blind, what did they teach you, and did it help?" I asked. He responded thoughtfully,

Well, I remember they said I didn't need to learn Braille because they thought my eyesight was good enough not to need it. They felt I would be able to read and make out the large print and do alright. While there at the School for the Blind, they had books that were created in large print, so I did read out of those books while I was there those two years. However, it did give me headaches from time to time and seemed to put a strain on my eyes. When I got back, though, the classes we had at school did not really have the larger print in the books we had for our lessons, so I could not read them. It was just a big blur of letters together. I did not want to go back up to St. Louis for school because I did not feel it really helped me at all. Also, I felt I needed to help Dad and Mom out as much as possible, and I was away from my family.

"Without access to enlarged material for school, how did you do the required schoolwork to get through school?"

Mom helped us all with our lessons. She would read each one of our lessons to us, and we would have to remember all that she had read to us. Then we would go back the next day and present our answers orally to the teachers. There were times when Mom would write down our answers if she could, and we would take that to school the next day.

Learning to See Through Blinded Eyes

I ended up with an overall "S average" [the equivalent of a "B average" in today's system] all through school and graduated from high school. I felt that was pretty good for this old fella. In fact, all of us kids graduated from high school.

Inquisitively I asked dad, "Who taught you what you needed to do when your eyesight kept declining?"

The whole time, I had to learn many things on my own. I had to learn to adapt to the changes in my eyes and try hard to remember what they looked like before my eyes changed.

I ingrained a mental picture of what things looked like and where they were. I also began to rely on my other senses since I could not always rely on my eyes. Developing them took lots of time and practice, but I did it.

Now, Mom did read the lessons, but I had to work hard to memorize the stuff. Dad would teach us things on the farm, but I had to adapt to not relying on my sight since it failed me too often, especially the worse it got.

I worked hard at keeping things around the house and farm in the same locations so I could get to it quicker. I allowed my ears to be my guide a lot, and I paid close attention to the pitch and tone of each object and person.

These times with my dad were precious to me. I continued to ask the many questions in my heart, loving the conversations they led to. "Did you learn to write? How did you learn to write?" He replied,

I did write some for a while. However, it became harder to write as my eyesight deteriorated. I had to have someone show me where the lines were so I could try to write in between the lines.

After a while, I just did not write but had others write for me unless I was signing my name. I did learn to sign my name in cursive.

At one time, it was pretty good, but I don't know about what it looks like now.

At least I remember how to spell it.

"Dad, how did you do math work?"

Arithmetic? I learned to do that in my head.

It may have taken me longer to do it, but I would visualize the blackboard in my head and how the numbers would line up and then add them in my head.

I would go over it to remember how the numbers added up and multiplied and divided. It was easier to get into 5s or 10s and then go from there.

Now when it came to money, I had to learn to keep my money in order. I had ones in the front of my wallet, then fives, and so on. I would memorize what I had in my wallet at all times.

"Dad, how was it going through grade school?" (That is what Dad called it, but now it would be called *elementary school*.)

Well, it wasn't too bad when I could go up to the blackboard and read the words and work my arithmetic.

I was just glad to be learning my lessons.

It became harder to read and complete my work after grade school, so I guess I would say grade school was pretty good. I could still see some letters and numbers, especially if they were big enough while I was in grade school.

It was a challenge when we switched schools from moving and such, but that was something I had to deal with. Learning new classmates, new teachers, and a new class set-up, but we got used to it pretty quickly. The teachers and my classmates also got used to us pretty quickly.

We had a lot of fun with our classmates for sure. We played games a lot and did a lot of running races, which I was really good at.

My favorite was playing pranks on the others. Oh, how I enjoyed doing a little scaring and pestering, too, especially the girls.

"Did it get harder through high school with all of you having eyesight issues?" I questioned.

It was a lot of time for us to complete our lessons cause Mom had to go over each one of our lessons by reading them. Mom read each one, and then like I said before, we had to memorize what we needed to know and then go back to our classes and tell our teachers the answers. Until our time with Mom, we would either be working with Dad on other things or listening to each other's lessons and helping each other with them. It was a lot of work for Mom, but she always helped us and pushed us to learn our lessons. As far as the work for the lessons, the teachers would work with us and allow us to do what we could do orally lots of the time.

The classmates were already used to us. High School was alright, I would say. I didn't really know there was much of a difference to tell you if it was too hard or if we were treated like we were retarded or anything like that. I never felt it was too hard; I just did what the teachers told me to do and made it through with a diploma. I am pretty proud of that one. I did long to go to college and become a history teacher because I loved learning about history so much. I could sit for hours and learn about all of it. *I would soak up history like a sponge on a hot day in a tub of cold water.*

"Who helped you the most through school?" I asked. Dad answered thoughtfully,

> Well, there were many people. The teachers over the years were understanding and would try to make things bigger so I could attempt to see it.
>
> The teachers made sure that the arithmetic was lined up just right so I could do the problems. I still had to figure out a lot of it in my head and did it the majority of the time. I ended up with pretty good grades.
>
> The teachers did a lot of lecturing, which helped since I was used to listening instead of relying on reading it myself. That seemed to give my eyes a break when they would lecture.
>
> There were a couple of classmates that were always helping me when I was at school as well. Some would be willing to write for me if I needed it, or I would just answer out loud, and the teacher would count that as my answer.
>
> Of course, Mom was always helping at home. Vonetta did as well; while she was still at home, she would read our lessons occasionally when Mom was focused on other things at the time.
>
> Vonetta could use her magnifier and read the lessons, so that did help. Vonetta was older, so she was not around for all our school years, especially to help with the younger two.

Then I asked a few more personal questions, "What was the hardest part of going through school with failing eyesight?"

Besides not seeing all the words and numbers to do my lessons, I would say not being able to see the faces of my classmates and people around me. Not being able to see the details that others could see—that would have been nice to see.

I had to have people describe the details and try to pull from memory what that looked like from when I was able to see it as a very young child.

That is still one of the hardest things. I could see people's outlines and estimate their height by their outlines. I created what I thought they looked like with details based on their voice, tone, and sound. I don't know if that is what they really looked like, but it is what they looked like to me.

As you know, I enjoy listening to my books all the time, but it would have been nice to read the books with my own eyes. Pictures books would be fuzzy, so I would have to create my own vision of what it was portraying.

I also would have liked to be able to read music since I like to sing and play the bass. I am not very good at it, but I pick and wallow from time to time. [Author's note: I will add that my dad is an amazing singer, and he plays the bass very well.]

I continued, "Did your peers take advantage of you being blind at school?"

Well, you always have those rascals that think they are funny. But I was always pulling pranks on others, so they eventually left me alone about it. I had no problems having a good time and making jokes with others. I had great classmates overall. Sometimes they would try to outsmart me by something, but as I learned to use my other senses, they didn't get by me very often.

Lots of times, I could sense them coming to try to get me, and then I would get them. Those were fun times because they did not expect me to do that. I could sneak up on them as a lion on a gazelle. I remember one time there were a couple of boys thinking that they could take Jewell and me, but we whooped up on them sure enough. They never tried that again and warned others who even mentioned it not to mess with us two.

My dad laughed hard after telling me about that account. I also knew that my dad was taught to always stay busy doing work. He was taught that work was important. We continued our conversations about the various jobs he had:

When I worked at the sawmill, there was an electric switch towards the end of the roller that if there was too much coming down on the roller that I could not manage, I could flip that switch to stop the roller. I tried to keep up as much as possible, but there were times I had to flip that switch. Then I would stack the lumber or put it over on the end trim or whatever. Everything there was done by hand.

Once in a while, we had a really big log and had to go up and turn the log. Then we had to put it on the carriage so we could run it through the big saw. Sometimes it took a little extra help to get it flat side down, and sometimes it did not. I did not mess around the big saw because it was electric, and I did not bother around it at all.

The edger had handles on it to where we could cut 2 x 4's or 2 x 6's. I would get the boards from the edger and would move them over a little bit. I could tell whether they were full-length or partial-length and then adjust the cutoff saw by turning the handle back to an even foot. Then I could put it over on the cutoff saw. I could handle that pretty good. Then the logs went out on a chain, and when the chain got full, the logs would get stacked in the bins. That is how we done it.

In the wintertime, there was always people coming to get slabs to take home to burn them. People would even come to get the spread-out sawdust for bedding for the cows or horses. We used a lot of sawdust ourselves when we lived on Pine Street. We put it up against the foundation of the house for more insulation because it was so cold.

Another job I would do at the lumber yard was load the lumber onto the people's trucks. Then I would tell Aunt Phoebe how many logs I had loaded for them. She would come out with a red keel to mark the logs. She moved it across the board like a crayon. She would count every board and mark them, and every once in a while, the people would try to say I did not get enough on there. But since she counted and checked me, they did not pull one over on us.

If there was someone that wanted a specific size of log, it was a challenge for me to do that, so others that worked there would have to do that part. I mean, I would try my best to get it as close as possible but couldn't always get it just right, like if they wanted something like a 10-foot log.

Sometimes I had to write down figures at the lumber yard, but it was hard for others to read what I wrote. After some time, they learned how I wrote it and figured it out.

Now when I worked at Little Stinkers [a bait company], I helped mix up the catfish bait. We had to mix up flour, molasses, fat, and bone meal [fish meal]. We would dump it all in a 55-gallon barrel. We would unload the molasses barrels that were about half full. Then we dumped the 55-pound bags of flour into the molasses.

Next, we put this electric motor with like a big fan on the bottom of it in the barrel and get that mixed just right. Then we put chicken fat in there. After that, we put what was like little pieces of meal and got it all mixed up. Then we put it in a big hopper over this machine that was run by air. You pushed this pedal, and it would push a certain amount of that mixture down in a tube. It would be weighed to get the right amount in the tubes.

I helped most with the lifting of the heavy stuff and helped with the mixing of stuff together. I also had to check to make sure every single tube was sealed and then put six of them in a carton. I used the taper and folded the ends down. I would then pull that tape over the ends of the carton and seal it up.

I would stack several hundred of them on a pallet until the pallet was full. After that, I would wrap the pallet with plastic, tape it all down, and push it up next to the door so that when the trucks came to get a load, it would be close for them to get. I enjoyed working there despite the smell. It was good getting to work with good friends, and it helped us with some money as well. It also helped me get away from your mother's nagging some too.

"Dad, what were some things you wished you could have *fully* seen?" (His two answers, along with his photograph, were incorporated into the cover of this book as a tribute.)

Learning to See Through Blinded Eyes

When we went to Colorado and went to the mountains! That was always one of my favorite places to go—to the mountains. I remember some specific details of what they looked like when I was younger and we lived there.

I also liked going to a field of wheat and watching the wind blow and seeing the wave that it created over the wheat. That is a beautiful sight to see.

Like those mountains and the wheat fields, I wondered if my dad created pictures of people and things in his mind, especially when he would read or be read to. It is extraordinary how my dad says he *sees* things:

Many times, I would create pictures in my mind. Especially if someone came into the shop or to the farm that I had not seen in a long time. I would pull up a picture of them in my mind to what I remember them as I seen them last. I would often create pictures when people were telling stories and especially when I was reading. You know how I always asked you girls to describe in detail? That is why. I had created pictures in my mind of all these things and people, so I wanted to be able to pull it up in my mind. Kind of like a file I kept on everything. Now when it came to reading, I for sure created pictures.

Like when the Word said details about the walls and how big they were, I could picture all of that in my mind. I would picture the characters of the Word and create what I thought they looked like.

"Dad, since you had your sight when you were little and could only see shapes and shadows as I grew up, what about colors?

Now I always seemed to have trouble with colors. Some colors I could see pretty good, like yellow or red. Sometimes green if it was a dark green. Of course, I could see white. [With] different shades of pink, I could see some of them. I would try to make sure you girls were wearing those colors so I could spot you easier as you were around the farm. I had trouble, especially with blues and browns.

I really liked the fall when I could see more of the colors come out on the trees. Sometimes if the sun was shining really brightly and there wasn't as many clouds in the sky, I could see a bit better. I seemed to be able to see the variation of light as something passed between my eyes and the sun. I could make it out better on those brighter days. I guess that was about all I can think about on the colors.

Now when I was sitting up on the 300 (tractor), I was up higher and seemed to be able to see better than if I was lower. There were times that I could see pretty good and other times that I just couldn't see. It frustrated me often because I could not see far enough down the road. I learned to adjust when I was doing things like driving by slowing down. I began to rely on my other senses. I used my hands and feet a lot to help. I paid attention to the vibrations of things, like the vibrations in the floor.

"You mean you could tell by the vibration of the floor who it was that was approaching?" I asked.

Well, when you would come in the house, you had a unique walk and step, so I could tell which of you girls it was coming in the door. All four of you girls had a different vibration and sound as you entered the house. If I were in the living room and saw the door open and saw you come in, I would identify you by your shade and shape. You know, each person has a specific walk and sound specific to them.

My dad continued to talk about his way of identifying people by the vibration of their walk on the floor. He told me about a relative who frequently came into the shop while Dad worked at the lumber yard. He would open the door, step one foot in, putting that foot down on the floor with a certain sound. Then he would bring in the other foot and put it down but with a different sound, as if to say, "I am here now. Now, what do you want?" This was every single time this relative would enter a room. Dad taught me that every-one seems to have a pattern of how they enter a place and walk, so when you learn each person's walk and sound, you can identify them just as if you saw them come in.

Although I grew up observing the miraculous ways he navigated life and learned so much through his patterns and mannerisms, I was still so curious and delighted to have these conversations. "Dad, you said that each person had a different sound. Did they have a different smell too?"

Oh yes, oh yes, they do. If a person smoked, I could tell immediately. I could tell by the [smell of the] different brands of cigarettes or cigars who it was most of the time. Even a woman's perfume, I could use to identify them. Your mom liked White Diamond, which to me, smelled good.

I can even tell when someone's scent (that I am familiar with) comes in contact with someone else because it changes your scent when you are around them. For example, when you go talk with someone who has smoked, it changes your scent when you come back in the house. I can smell your scent, but [now it is] mixed with someone else's.

For men, I could sometimes tell [who it is] by their hair stuff or their shaving stuff. I think because my sense of smell was so strong, I did not like using much on me but some Vaseline in my hair. Many of those things are too strong and smell awful, so I just won't use them. I don't want to walk around smelling like a took a bath in all that stuff.

Learning to See Through Blinded Eyes

Remembering that my dad has a great sense of direction, I questioned Dad on that too! It astounds me how he navigates, though legally blind, seeing through blinded eyes! Dad says,

It just was automatic to me. I learned and memorized everything. I learned by the sun's movements to determine where north, south, east, and west were and kept that in perspective everywhere we went. I learned to keep that as my focus and build a map in my mind of where everything was in relation to each other. When we would go places, I would try to memorize each curve and hill so that if we went there again, I could get there and get back. So, it eventually was just automatic for me. Especially here on the farm.

I want to close up this chapter, *Conversations with Dad*, with our conversation about music. Although my dad is modest about his abilities with music, as I noted earlier in this chapter, he is a good singer and plays the bass guitar very well. I knew there had to be something that enabled him to sing and play bass without the sighted ability to read music. Here is the rest of that story:

Just as I memorized my lessons, I memorized music. It was easy to hear the various tones and pitches. Then I learned to pay close attention to what others were singing and playing; I picked up the bass and began to pick at it a little bit. I do not play that well, but I enjoy it a whole lot!

As far as songs, I had to listen to the words. The words of a song are particularly important. If there was someone who was leading and did not enunciate the words well, I could get the words messed up. It would get me frustrated when others would not enunciate. Words are so important to hear. If I was able to get the melody or harmony, it wasn't enough without the correct words. It is vital to enunciate when you speak, but especially when you sing.

I love singing and harmonizing. I love to worship and sing praises to the Lord. He deserves our worship. He deserves our praise. Oh, how I love Jesus!

Dad-isms and humor...

"Hey, Rachel, what is that over there?"

I would look and not see anything different than before and reply. "Dad, I don't see anything different."

He would reply, "Me neither. I was just a checking. Even if it was different, I wouldn't see it either" (with a big grin on his face and chuckle).

Chapter Four
Family Ties

My dad spent almost all his time with his family on the farm. They kept the farm going with crops, horses, cattle, and chickens. Even when they lived in a different location, they would go to his Grandpa Alonzo's place (the Lockard farm) to help them do whatever was needed. My dad recalls many times working to keep the cows milked. He reminisced,

> Dad had a stroke or something when he was younger, which left him weakened in his body, and he never was as strong after that. But he kept working. Us boys and even Wilma would help milk. We would set out around eleven ten-gallon cans of milk every other day.
>
> If it wasn't raining, we had electricity to run the milking machine. If it was showering, the electricity would come and go, and we would have to hook the hose up to the tractor and let it idle. We had weights put on the hose to the milking machine to where there was just the right amount of pressure to create

about the same pressure pulling when the electricity was working. That way, the heifer's udders were not damaged, and the milking could still be done. There were times we had to do it by hand, but that took lots more time for sure.

We had a big milk cooler where we could fit close to ten of those ten-gallon cans of milk at one time. Sometimes we would pull one can out and set it out while we put a fresh can of warm milk in to cool it off. We would do this over and over to keep all the milk cool and not let it spoil. We made sure that the morning's milk was put in the cooler before the milk hauler would come so it would be cool and not spoil before he got there. Then we would have fresh cans that he would take and leave the empty cans with us. There were times we started milking at night. There would be times us kids did not get all of that done before the bus came, so that left Mom to deal with it. She would have to move those heavy cans into the cooler since we had to go to school.

My dad also learned how to build fences to keep the livestock in a specific area. He said that building fences was a challenge to learn because of the barbed wire. He quickly learned where to put his hands and handle the wire.

One time we had come back to Grandpa Alonzo's, and Dad had to go to Passaic to get some rolls of barbed wire. He came back with three rolls, and we had to put up that fence to keep Grandpa's cattle from getting over into Aunt Canny's property. We had to put up a fence because we were having to watch the cows and make sure they stayed over on Grandpa's land. Aunt Canny would pitch a fit if Grandpa's cows went even a little bit over on her land.

Once we built the fence, we did not have to watch the cattle as much until that one summer that was so dry and hot that everyone was running out of water. Down in the creek, there was a nice big spring. There was a group of three families that we would have to help with the cows so that these families could have some water for their cows. Our cows were usually about the last ones to get a drink since we had to stay and help the other families with their cows. The cows would get their drink, and we would bring them back up the lane to where the big pond is at.

This was a summer I was a little bitty kid. I remember it was on a Sunday because Grandpa Alonzo threw a massive fit. He hated to work on Sundays, but he had to get water for the cows. So, Grandpa went down to where the well was.

[Author's note: This well is still in the same location. It is just northeast of where I grew up and the same well I pumped water to carry up to the house. I will share more about that a little later on.]

Grandpa got down in the well, used some black powder, and set it off. There rushed up some water through there in a crack the blast had created. We took three-gallon buckets down there and some planks to lay across the well. We used rope, stood out on the boards, and drew up water in the buckets. Then we take it to the trough so the cows and horses would have something to drink. The only other water was the creek and the pond there by the well. It took us a long while, I cannot recall how long, but it was a while. We would have to keep drawing buckets and filling the trough for the cows and horses. Sometimes we had to chase some cows away so others could get a drink and then go back to drawing water to bring more.

My dad also learned how to tend to the garden. His dad and mom (my grandparents) taught him what to look for to ensure things were ripe and ready to harvest. He learned what to watch for on collecting eggs from the chickens. Grandma and Grandpa worked each day teaching their kids how to keep the farm going. They all worked together as a family to make all things work for them.

Another memory my dad shared of the farm was riding on the front of the oat seeding disc, pulled by a team of horses. As the team of horses got just south of the bridge, close to the house, something spooked them. My dad did not know what spooked the horses, but they suddenly took off running. He was little then, and the disc he was riding on kept catching the ground and throwing him around. He had to hold on to the disc for dear life. The disc did not detach but kept jostling him around until everyone could get the horses to calm down. He began listening to the sound of the disc and bracing for it to throw him around so he could hold on and not fall off. He acknowledged that the disc would have cut him to pieces if he had been thrown off. He said after that incident, he began learning more about the feel of the machinery parts and their specific sounds to help him in future events.

That disc riding story wasn't the only astounding activity my dad participated in! He learned to do many activities you might never imagine someone with visual impairment would do. For example, my Grandpa taught Dad how to shoot a gun! He began by having him shoot at bottles and cans first.

He would locate things with his eyes as best he could but did not rely fully on his sight since it progressively worsened. My dad's sense of direction was keen. And they didn't stop there. Grandpa Ralph and my dad's Grandpa Alonzo also taught him how to work on the tractor, what each part did, and how it all worked together.

Dad learned the sounds of each machine. Then he paid close attention to the sounds of when it was running correctly. He learned the sounds of each part and could tell when something was off by the sound and sometimes even by the smell of it. Dad recalled more than once, the sound from the vibration of the tractor tires on the ground alerted him that something was stuck in the tire. He would get off the tractor and feel around the tire until he could find what was in it. My dad would remove whatever it was, get back on the tractor, and go again.

Dad told me of a time that he knew that one of the dogs was in the chicken house:

I heard the cackling of the hens over and over and figured that something was wrong. When I ran over to the coup and was searching around, I kept hearing rustling and kept moving toward that sound. I saw a flash of black running from me and could smell that dog. I hollered at her and told her to get, and she did. After feeling around, I noticed that multiple eggs that should have been there for the collecting were not there. I put two and two together and figured out the dog was getting my eggs. That dog had to go for sure because I could not have an egg-eating dog around here.

Dad talked about how he learned so much from his mom and dad; they were such amazing parents who instilled the importance of family. He reminded me that he desired to attend college and be a history teacher. But my dad realized that Grandpa Ralph could not work the farm alone. He told me that he knew that staying around to help his family on the farm was what he needed to do.

While working the family farm, Dad would sometimes catch a ride into town with his cousins that lived farther out. Often it was to get to work at the lumber yard, but most of the time, my dad remained on the farm. It was with the help of these relatives that he made it to town for church, where he met Loretta Epperson, his future wife, and eventually, my mom.

I went to church with one of my cousins often, and Loretta went to the same church there in town. You know the old Assembly of God. Your mom was there in the CA [Christ Ambassador] group. So, I met her at church. I also knew about her because she was always riding around town with all her friends in her convertible. Boy, how she loved that convertible and riding around, especially when she could put the top down. Your mom had lots of friends. She always had lots of people around her. I would always hear them talking about her convertible when they were at church.

Did you know she was even dating another guy when we got together? But that ended pretty quick. I guess my good looks won her over. Your mom had beautiful shoulder-length hair and kept it so pretty. She would brush it often and kept it so nice, and it did not look like a rat's nest. That was impressive to me, and I was attracted to her because she kept herself so nice. She was always happy, and her laugh was so contagious. She would laugh at everything. I liked hearing her laugh; there was so much joy in her laugh. Loretta was always wanting to go places and see different sights.

I recall our first date. My cousin wanted to go down to see Martha but did not want to go alone, so he asked if I would go with him. I did not think just two fellas going down there was such a good idea, and I felt having a lady along would be better. So, I invited Loretta to go with us. I asked her if she would mind going down to see Martha with us and that… *it would be a little different*. She thought about it for a little bit and then said she guessed she would. We went down to the nuthouse in Nevada to see Martha, and that was our first date.

It was a lot of fun telling that to people when they asked us about our first date. I say I took her to the nuthouse and then laugh at the response of everyone who hears that. They often do not say anything or just clam up. That makes me laugh so hard even to this day.

You know, we always had two or three people along with your mom and me, when we went places. They seemed to like to ride in Loretta's convertible. We would go down to Nevada sometimes and even to Rich Hill. So, there wasn't many times I remember it just being us by ourselves. I also don't remember when we decided to be a couple. I know it was a short time after we went down to the nuthouse[4], though. I remember Loretta brought me home one night after a CA Rally, and it was super late. Our relationship just kind of grew from there.

Not many girls were in school at the same time Dad attended school. Although he still recalls a couple of girls he felt kept their hair pretty, and he still remembers their names.

But Dad said Mom was always fun to be around and was the one who caught his attention. He also liked her a lot because she was always at church. "You can have a great time at church and with the church folk, but you have to be willing to just be yourself around them. Not some stiff-necked person who does not think a Godly person can have fun."

Dad and Mom married on August 12, 1966. They were married at the Butler First Assembly of God church, where they met. They bought a house in town and began their life together.

It was not even three years into their marriage when they were blessed with the arrival of their first-born daughter on June 15, 1969. My older sister Christine was their pride and joy. Dad recalls her arrival and early years:

> Chris was one of the most beautiful babies I
> had ever laid eyes on. It was like a bright light shone

down on her to make her radiant. She was okay for a little while, but then we started noticing she was very sickly. Doctors' visits came more frequent, and we had to learn how to take care of her to help her stay alive. The doctors did not expect her to live a year with Cystic Fibrosis and warned us that having more children was a risk. We trusted the Lord to help us with her, and He sure did.

We learned how to give her "beating treatments" [that is where my dad would lay Chris over his lap and use his hands to lightly beat on her back to loosen up the phlegm in her lungs so she could breathe better]. I had to learn to listen to her breathing to see if she needed a treatment. While I was giving her beating treatments, I had to listen to her cough to see if it was bringing up what was needed.

Loretta had to stop working and began babysitting since she was always running to doctor's appointments and hospital stays. We had to monitor Chris all the time and make sure she was getting everything she needed. Chris was a miracle, and we celebrated each and every year she was here with us.

When we lived in town, we were always going out to the farm to help Dad and Mom with whatever they needed. Chris loved being out on the farm. Oh, how my mom [Grandma Rachel] loved Chris. She loved her coming out to the farm, hanging around as she cooked and worked in the garden.

Then, of course, eight years later, you came along, and you kind of know the rest from there. Little did we know you were going to be the biggest handful of all!

When I asked Dad what the hardest thing was about raising us was, he told me the hardest thing was just that…

[It was] raising you girls and making sure that you had clothes on when we had company! Generally, you girls would have clothes on, but there were times when you would just rather run around in your underwear outside without a care in the world.

Also, I had to make sure *you* [speaking directly to me] were not getting into things you were not supposed to get into, which was most of the time. You kept me on my toes for sure. We decided to move out to the farm when you were just one year old to help Dad take care of it since Mom died in '76. I had to teach you girls how to take care of things. Raising girls was hard enough, but when I had to raise girls to work and run a farm, it made it harder. You girls had to learn things that I would have loved to had boys for. But I had four sassy, strong daughters that I had to teach and train. I guess God wanted me to have a challenge, so he gave me four stubborn, hardheaded girls that kept me always having to find them, correct them, teach them, and train them. Especially you, Rachel Ruth. You challenged me the most with your questions, always wanting to know how and why. You always seemed to get yourself in trouble with your mouth and questioning. Not to mention all the times you were pestering Chris or Esther. Boy, you were something else for sure!

As I look back on it, I am so thankful to the Lord for you girls. I always tried to raise you girls to work hard and see things in a different way. I wanted my girls to be able to make it better than most girls. You can survive and thrive. I wanted to make sure that my girls were strong girls that knew that they could make it with the Lord. [To know that] no matter what obstacles you all faced, you would be victorious because God was with you. I did what I could to train you girls well. I hope that I trained you all to make sure that you always put things back in their spot, especially the tools. You always need to have your tools right where you can get them. You do not need tools just thrown in a bucket or laid on the ground somewhere [then] you don't know where you left them. [Yes, my dad did always harp on putting his tools back in their place.]

I always wanted my girls to learn things and be kind to people. I wanted you to remember that family is especially important and still is, at least to me. Things can come and go, but **family ties** are what hold people together. I may not have relayed that as I wanted to, but I sure meant to.

Dad-isms and farm-life...

"The best fertilizer is not bought in the store. It is fresh from the backside of the cow deposited on my garden."

Anytime we pass by a stockyard, Dad would take the biggest whiff in and say, "Smell all of that money!"

Chapter Five
Learn Your Lessons

When you are little, you do not really notice how different you are from others. It seems that as you get older, you begin to notice the differences between you and your peers. Perhaps you stand out as dressing differently. Or maybe you believe differently or carry yourself differently, and so on. Then you begin to ask yourself questions about why you are different. I asked this several times beginning early on in elementary school. It seemed every other kid in my class was enjoying playing video games and experiencing new things like color television, lunch boxes at school, car phones, washers and dryers in their house, and air conditioning.

All these things were foreign to our family, not just the new conveniences but even basics like running water. Our family was used to completing all the outside chores with the garden, animals, and yard daily before completing homework and reading at bedtime. Our daily routine included carrying water from our well in a five-gallon bucket to the house over and over to have water to cook with, take a bath, or even flush the toilet. To flush the toilet without running water, we had to bring in buckets of water and pour water slowly as the toilet was flushing to force down the sewage. Then we would leave a little water in the toilet bowl for the next use. I know it sounds gross, but we did not flush after every use because it would mean carrying more buckets of water to the house. Our family was also accustomed to counting our steps to the outhouse if we needed to use it at night.

So as a child, those were some of the ways I began to recognize that my upbringing differed from that of many other children in our community. Since my father was blind my entire life, he taught us differently.

My earliest memory of this was when I was helping Dad change a spark plug on one of the machines. He dropped the spark plug on the ground and bent down to retrieve it. Dad said, "I know it hit the ground and bounced to the north, so I know I am getting close." He began to feel around for it in the area he felt he heard it land. I stood there and watched him use his hands to locate the spark plug within moments with no assistance, wondering how it was that he knew which direction it bounced.

Being an inquisitive child, I asked my dad how he knew where it was. He explained that he had pulled the machine onto a big piece of cardboard to make his repairs. So, when the spark plug fell, he could hear where it bounced by the sound it made as it struck the cardboard underneath. Then he heard it hit again with a different sound, in a different location and could pinpoint its direction by listening to the sound it made. It was amazing to me even then.

Over the years, I continued to be in awe of how he managed to complete task after task, making so many things he did look effortless.

Being a *Daddy's girl*, I followed him around everywhere he went. My older sister, Christine, would help from time to time but couldn't assist on the farm much since she had Cystic Fibrosis. So being the next to the oldest, I was chosen to help Dad with whatever needed to be done around the farm. Farm work consisted of helping feed the pigs, gathering eggs, feeding the chickens, checking on the cattle and horses, bailing hay, mowing the lawn, tending to the garden, doing the laundry with the old-time ringer washer, gathering milk from the milking cows, and carrying buckets of water to the house when needed. Dad could accomplish all these chores easily and had the most amazing way of handling each thing.

I remember vividly being so intrigued by how my dad walked around the farm without even using a cane or holding onto someone. Multiple times, sometimes several times in a day, I tried to do it exactly like he did. With my eyes closed, I would count my steps and try to sense where I was by sounds and smells. I was not very successful at doing this! I even tried squinting (opening my eyes just a tiny bit) to see if I could manage to get around better that way. I found that it was way harder to do than I had even imagined. I would practice and practice and did not seem to come anywhere close to how my dad was able to do it. He was inspiring to watch as he moved around the farm and avoided obstacles like nothing was even there.

Daddy's Eyes

Dad always said that I was a stinker when I was growing up. (That is what some might call a little rascal or prankster.) I still smile at the thought, knowing he was completely right! I would try to set obstacles in his way or do things just to see how he would respond. I would do things to see if I could trip him up in some fashion. For example, I would move his tools to a different spot, somewhere close but not in the exact spot Dad always had them in. He would go out to find his tools (which he always left in the same spot), and he would feel where they were supposed to be and then get upset and start feeling around to see where it was. He would find it quickly and then holler at me, and of course, I would get into trouble!

Another example of how I would try to fool Dad was the time I got into my mom's perfume. I remember spraying it all around in the back room. He came in the front door and hollered at me, asking me if I had sprayed the perfume. I lied and said I didn't. He asked again, and of course, I lied again. I can hear him now as if it were yesterday. He came to the back room where I was and said, "Rachel Ruth do you think I am stupid? I may be blind, but I can smell like nobody's business! Yes, you did spray perfume all over this room—and it stinks to high heavens! Get yourself prepared for a belting."

I was corrected or, as Dad likes to refer to it, "getting it from my head to my brain." It always amazed me how he saw it was me and never my other three sisters. Do you know the saying "teachers have eyes in the back of their heads"? I never could figure out how Dad, being blind, could see so much, but he would always see what was going on!

Learning to See Through Blinded Eyes

Learning Dad's way of doing things around the farm was the coolest thing and the most frustrating part of growing up all at the same time. For example, when it came to driving the tractor, Dad taught me how to hear the ground against the tires to see (know) where I was on the farm or on the road. There is a certain pitch and feel that would determine where we were. For instance, if the sound of the tire was changed a certain way, I was getting too close to the edge of the pond or ditch area. He had all the farm areas memorized by the sound of each section, so he could navigate it all without difficulty.

When we planted the garden, Dad would have us place a stake at one end of the row. Then, he would walk down to the other end and put a stake down there. Dad would know that he was at the other end by the feel of the ground changing beneath his feet. Then he would take twine, tie it to that side where he was, walk it back down to where we were, and have us tie it on that stake. Next, he would take two big steps east, and we would do another row. That is how the entire garden was staked.

Our main garden was a full acre of land, and we did this all the way down the garden. When it was done, it was time to plow the rows. Dad would get out his plow, place it right up against the tightly tied twine, and walk the plow down the row without any issues. I watched him do this time and time again with ease. He would feel the pull of the twine against the plow and know he was exactly right. I tried it a couple of times and realized the genius in it. Then we used a special machine to plant seed. It had a rotating wheel that spaced the seeds out just right as we walked along the plowed row. The twine would remain so he would know where the plowed row was to plant the seeds within the row. If the starting was from a plant rather than a seed, then my dad would place one hand in the row facing north and south and the other hand right up against it facing east and west. This was how he determined the distance apart for each plant. Our family garden was a prized garden for sure. It seemed like we grew some of everything on that acre. Our tomatoes were some of the best in the area. Our watermelons, cantaloupes, and pumpkins often won prizes at the fairs. People were always coming out to the farm to buy our prize-winning produce. There were many times that our prized produce was written about in the local newspaper.

(My sister and I with some of the produce.)

The gathering of the harvest was an amazing process with Dad as well. He taught me how to judge whether the produce was ripe by the sound it made when thumped and by the feel and smell of the produce. He would listen for the sound it made when he would thump it, and Dad would have me listen to what it sounded like as he taught me to differentiate when it was and wasn't ripe. With corn, he taught me to feel the outside of the stalk and the corn husk. It was ripe and ready to pick if it felt firm, and you could feel the rows just right. He would have me smell the difference between a fully ripened vegetable and one that was not. For each vegetable, there was a difference in smell and feel between the ones that were ready to harvest and those that needed to ripen more.

This was a hard lesson for me to learn because I was trying to use my eyes and not all my other senses.

Other times in the **learn your lessons** process, Dad would ask me what it would look like, and I would have to describe it in extreme detail. Dad wanted things described with extreme detail so he could envision what I was describing and tell me what it was by my description. This was like a game to me when I was younger. I enjoyed finding things that I was unfamiliar with, taking them to him, and describing what it was. He would feel it and smell it, and then Dad would shoot back exactly what it was with such precision.

One of my favorite memories was when I found an old glass-cutting tool. I had no idea what it was, so I asked Dad. He asked me to first describe it. I said, "It is about six inches in length, and on one end, it has a small round disc with small groves around it. That disc rotates when you run it over something. On the other end, it has a smooth round ball-like thing." He said it was a glass-cutting tool but wanted to feel it to make sure. I handed it to him so he could feel the object. After he felt it, he confirmed that he was correct. He proceeded to tell me how they used it in the olden days. As I look back at those many moments, it seems that he wanted to envision the tool before he felt it. The details he taught me to give with everything enabled him to envision what it was before he could feel it.

Dad also learned to adapt so that he could take care of the animals. With the milking cows, he would take the bucket and place his thumb down the first knuckle over the edge.

Dad knew the bucket was full when the milk hit the tip of his thumb, because it was then about an inch from the top.

When we dealt with the chickens, it took me longer to learn how he did it because I wanted to automatically use my sight. He taught me to first listen to the chickens in the coop before I entered. For instance, if they seemed unsettled and were moving around a lot, or if you could hear them crying out in fear, you would know there was a predator nearby. When this occurred, it often signaled that there was at least one snake in the coop! Dad would first go in, moving slowly, listening to the chickens' movements, and then listen for movement by the snake. He would then move toward the snake slowly, bend down, and grab the snake by the tail. My dad could tell where the snake was heading by the sound and direction of the snake's movement. I could see it all unfolding and would often be alarmed! But Dad had taught me not to shout out where it was or make lots of noise to frighten the chickens even more.

Because Dad relied on his hearing to help him see (perceive and interpret important information), he wanted it quiet until he was done with the task. When he was performing specific tasks that required his complete concentration, he only wanted me to speak or tell him things when I was to do so. (I should include here that remaining silent while he was catching snakes in the chicken coop wasn't one of my strengths. I received many beltings for not heeding that training.) Dad also taught me how to grab a chicken and chop off its head. He had an old stump located northeast of

Grandpa's house that we used for this. It was also just west of the chicken coop, which made it easier. He would grab the chicken and take it over to the old stump that already had the machete in it. He would grab the machete and stretch the chicken's neck out on the stump, then hold it with one hand right at the base of the neck. Next, he would swing the machete and chop off the head of the chicken. He would let the chicken flop around and listen while it flopped. He would then go and pick it up and take it to Mom to de-feather and cook up.

There are so many more things that Dad demonstrated and trained me on— things that one might never expect someone blind to do, much less teach someone else to do. One of my favorites to share is how he taught me to…DRIVE!

My dad first taught me to drive tractors around the farm. He taught me how to drive the trucks and the van. He taught me to listen to the road and tire as it hit the gravel and the asphalt and to hear the difference.

As I stated earlier, I was a bit of a stinker and would do things just as a joke to prank him. Well, I really did this with driving. I was one with a heavy foot and tended to speed every time I was behind the wheel. I often went faster than the speed limit just to see if he noticed, and, he did. When I asked how he knew, he said he could hear it!

When Dad rode with me anywhere, if, or I should say, when he sensed that I was speeding, he would say, "Rachel Ruth, you are speeding! Slow down to the speed limit right now."

Learning to See Through Blinded Eyes

Here is one of my recollections of learning just how well my Dad could hear pitch: When I reached my driving years, we had an old Ford 1970s van with a *doghouse* (an engine with a cover over it like a doghouse) in between the driver's and passenger's seats. That vehicle did not have power steering, power brakes, or power anything else! The doghouse added lots of extra heat to the van's interior. To make matters worse, it did not have air conditioning either. So our windows were always down, especially in the summer and spring. I am giving these details to say… this did not help my cause at all! My dad knew the certain pitch that the tires made when driving on the road at 55 mph. So, when I would speed, the pitch would change, and with the windows always down, he could hear it every time. That is how he could tell I was speeding and by how much—by the pitch!

Dad also taught me how to parallel park. He would have mom pull right up next to the car parked immediately in front of our parking space and then get out. Dad would get in the van. He had me stand right next to the vehicle behind the parking space he was attempting to park into. I would stand at that vehicle's front passenger side headlight and begin talking to Dad. He would listen to me talk and be able to turn the wheels just right to fit the vehicle in the parking spot. It was sad to say, but my legally blind father could parallel park better than my sighted mother!

When it came to vehicles, he wanted me to know how to use my other senses to notice when something was not right. For instance, he taught me to know when the tires on a vehicle were separating solely by the feel and sound of the tires. I could call him and describe the sound of what was going on in my vehicle, and, sure enough, he could pinpoint the issue. Almost always, when I would take it to the shop or have someone look at it, their assessment would confirm he was exactly right.

Living on a farm, we always had critters that would come around. Dad wanted all of us to be prepared for anything. He wanted us all to be as independent as possible. Because all these critters were lurking about, Dad taught me how to shoot. He started by placing cans in a line on the ground. Then he told us in detail how to hold the BB gun, locate the sight, and get it just right before pulling the trigger. Dad was an amazing shot.

One of my favorite memories of Dad's shooting expertise occurred late one evening when I was a teenager. My bed was in the living room, and I heard the commotion of animals outside. Dad came to the living room because the racket also woke him up. He had a shotgun in his hand and told me to be quiet. He stepped onto the porch, intently listening to the movements of a coyote, who by then was super close to the house. (Of course, curious me, I followed him out there. It was one of those times to remain perfectly silent as he had trained me to be.)

I remember he pause, listened, and then adjusted his body and the shotgun. He did this a couple more times before he pulled the trigger. Bang! And then I heard this yelp and was in shock that he had hit it!

I marveled at the shot as we went back inside. "How in the world were you able to do that?" I asked. He said he first had to listen to hear the exact direction the sound was coming from. Then he had to hear the distance it was from where he was.

Next, he explained how he had to adjust the gun to point its firing position to be about the height of an average coyote. I was blown away that he had studied all these things to the point that he could shoot in the dark and hit his target. Even growing up, being endlessly amazed at his abilities, this is one time that I could not fully comprehend how he was able to accomplish such a feat. To me, the darkness was impossible to overcome. But to him, it was not much different than when it was light outside. He always amazed me.

There are so many examples of how Dad taught me to use other senses to adapt and complete any given task. Just using my sight was not an option when I was growing up. Dad wanted us to be able to survive should any of us lose one of our senses. He prepared us by training all of our senses.

It was never good enough to just see it with our physical eyes or to state simple facts without description. He wanted us to be so skilled at describing things in such detail that anyone else could envision what we could see, hear, feel, and/or smell.

So, while he was to some a man labeled with a disability, to me, Dad was a man with super abilities that could outrun us all and do things better than most sighted people could, even those with perfect 20/20 vision.

Dad-isms and driving...

Mom was known for slowing down when she was talking while driving. On one such trip, I was reading all the road signs to Dad, and a sign said, "Slower Traffic Keep Right." Dad piped up and said, "Loretta, you go any slower, and you are gonna have to drive on the shoulder."

Chapter Six
See the Ability
(Not the Disability)

More often than not, I saw my dad as having *super abilities* rather than a disability. Even though, according to classmates or even the medical field, he was labeled as having a disability. He had the special license plate and the placard hanging on the rear-view mirror, signifying he had a disability. He had a special identification card since he could not pass a driver's test. Dad carried a special pass to get into all the national parks for free because of this labeled "disability."

It was normal for me to attend blind conventions and blind camps as I was growing up. I met so many people that had varying degrees of visual impairments. Some were totally blind, some legally blind, some both blind and deaf, and some had a visual impairment paired with a mental disability.

I can recall time and time again when I was blown away at the abilities they possessed to adapt to a world without using their physical eyes. It was as if they could combine their other senses and create a better picture of what was there than a sighted person could.

At these camps and conventions, there were sighted people as well. They were the ones who drove or were family members of the visually impaired people. I am thankful that I was one of those who got to have such unique experiences. I learned how to play spoons at blind camp using Braille cards. I also remember watching some of these men and women go tubing down the river without any fear. Their ability outshines their disability over and over.

For instance, a normal game of shuffleboard for a sighted person seemed simple. You look down at the other side, take your stick up against the puck, judge how much force you need to use to push, and then shove it down to the other end. For a person with a visual impairment, it took such skill. Someone on the other side tapped a shuffleboard pole on the middle of the "10" space several times for the person to hear where they were shooting for.

It had to be quiet while they concentrated on that sound and then adjusted their body, stick, and puck in the direction of the sound. When they shoved it down, they wanted a report of how close they were to the "10." They wanted descriptive details on whether it was too far left or right, too short, or too long of a shot. This gave them a sense of how to change their approach for the next time. They also wanted to know details about where their opponents' pucks were too. The game that should have taken a short time to complete was extended because of all the extra components involved. The skill level required for them to accomplish these tasks was amazing.

I recall multiple times at camp when it was game competition time that I just knew, since I had excellent vision, that I was going to wipe the floor with everyone else. (But I should have known from growing up with Dad that I was going to be in for a challenge like never before!) Let's just say I was beaten several times at shuffleboard.

Another game my dad loves to play is horseshoes. He would have me stand and tap the stake where he was to throw it. He would listen for the tapping and then throw. Of course, that was a slightly dangerous spot for me, but I learned quickly to get out of the way when he began throwing.

Marco Polo in the pool was an everyday feat for Dad, but he could swim and dive better than I could. He taught us girls early on how to swim. He wanted us to be able to get out of the water if we ever fell into it. So he purposely threw me into the water young and talked me through with details on exactly what I needed to do to get out. Knowing how to swim is vital when you live on a farm with ponds and creeks.

Another strong memory of mine is that my dad was a huge part of the Missouri Council of the Blind. He served as public relations chairman for many years. Then he served in various other positions on the council for over fifty years. In addition to the Missouri Council, he served on the American Council of the Blind. Because of his involvement, we had many opportunities to travel and meet all kinds of new people. These times of traveling to council meetings and conventions broadened my awareness of all the abilities of so many people with visual impairments. I saw firsthand how many adapted to the environment, developing ways to accomplish normal tasks that a sighted person might see as a "no brainer." For example, walking across crosswalks to a sighted person seems easy because they can see the changing of the traffic lights and notice the traffic flow. But that is a huge ordeal for someone with visual impairments. They cannot see when the light changes, the walking sign lights up, or the red hand flashes.

When we went to San Francisco, California, for the American Council of the Blind convention, we discovered that the city of San Francisco had installed some of their traffic lights with sound attached to the signals (accessible pedestrian signals). East and West crosswalks had different tones than the North and South crosswalks. It released a loud sound when it was time for someone to walk across and would get faster when the light was about to change to the red hand. It also had a countdown so you would know when the light was preparing to switch to the other traffic flow. When changing to the red hand, it had a long beep and three short beeps, which let anyone walking across know they had better hurry up. When the red hand, signifying that it was not appropriate for them to walk across, was visible, it was accompanied by a loud voice saying, "WAIT." The signals were also equipped with tactile buttons showing directions for the visually impaired.

As I stated before, we traveled all over with these conventions. We had been to other big cities previously and on vacations, yet we had never encountered that before.

Learning to See Through Blinded Eyes

I remember one of the times the state convention was held in Branson, Missouri. Dad, Mom, and a couple of others were instrumental in making things safer for the visually impaired to maneuver around the property. They visited in advance the hotel where the convention would be held later that year. They went around the hotel and found areas where the staff could make the property safer. They also instructed the management and staff to place braille everywhere there was signage (on all doors, directional signs, location of the ice machine, etc.). Even though Dad could not fully read Braille, he knew his numbers in Braille.

The team also visited different businesses and restaurants in Branson and located places that would best accommodate visually impaired visitors. This happened many times when they had a convention in Missouri at least once a year. I assume the American Council did the same since they always sent out a packet of recommended places to stay around the convention location. They also recommended restaurants and places to visit that were more accommodating for visually impaired visitors. No matter where we visited when I was still in school, I loved to look around to see if those locations had any cool safety measures, gadgets, Braille signs, or flashing lights for those with hearing or visual impairments. Sadly, most of the businesses and buildings we visited did not even have some of the gadgets or accommodations for the visually or hearing-impaired population. When you really take the time to think about it, those with visual impairments want to be as independent as possible—just like you and I do.

Providing them access through accommodations and modifications in these buildings and public places helps them feel that independence.

While at the conventions hosted by the American Council of the Blind, there were always vendor exhibits that highlighted the latest gadgets and aids that were designed for the visually impaired. I think I had more fun checking these exhibits out than Dad did. There was also a new advanced talking watch, which Dad was always interested in. He wanted to know the time at all times, but he wanted to hear clearly what the watch was saying. He would say, "I don't like that one because it sounds like someone from Canada," or "that won't help me cause that person is talking like they have mush in their mouth." We would play with every watch and clock in the exhibit until he found the ones he liked the best. There were talking calculators, Braille writing machines (which are super cool to see and so interesting to witness how they write and read braille), and games made for visually impaired people. To this day, I have Dad's chess set and checkers, which we played all the time. Dad beat me at chess every time we played, and most times when we played checkers.

Another one of my favorite memories of these conventions was watching movies. Yes, visually impaired people enjoy watching movies like everyone else! But they have access to special versions called audio-described movies. I have said for years that you have not lived until you have watched Forrest Gump (which seemed like a forever movie the first time I saw it without the descriptions) as an audio-described movie. These versions describe in detail the scenes and expressions of the characters, scene changes, and more. It makes the movie come alive so the visually impaired person can create a virtual movie reel in their mind as they are *watching* the movie. It also makes the movie much longer. When I watched it as an audio-described movie, I have to say it made me more aware of what was happening in the scenes than if I was watching it without the audio descriptions. Needless to say, I have never watched Forrest Gump again after that experience.

Going to the conventions helped me become more aware of what was out there for people with visual and hearing impairments. I began to see things differently everywhere I went. I began to see things from a different perspective. I observed that many places were working on accommodating wheelchair access. Still, many had not even considered the changes and updates needed for those with visual and hearing impairments. Living my whole life seeing and experiencing things from varied perspectives truly impacted who I am and even what I do now.

These experiences and others throughout my lifetime established a deep appreciation and respect for life and ministry. I developed a great desire to make a difference for others in the world around us. Today, in one of my roles in life, I am a Special Education Teacher. I am determined to help those labeled as *having disabilities* to capture their *abilities*, adapt, and become productive citizens. I want them and others to see that they all possess amazing abilities, can learn, and have great successes. My motto is, **"Everyone can accomplish great things."**

It bothers me greatly when I hear statements like: "They are retarded and can never learn. They are disabled and can never hold a job. Because they cannot hear, they obviously are too stupid to have a say." I am here to tell you that I have come across so many people that have a truly legitimate disability that would, to me, warrant a reason to feel sorry for themselves. Yet I have found they are some of the most determined people, determined to overcome and find another way of accomplishing great feats despite their disability. I still marvel at how they can play games better than me, find their way around places that they are unfamiliar with, dare to try something to eat when they cannot see what it is, or even compliment someone on their appearance just by that person's voice and tone.

Dad would be so encouraging to others, whom I could see were burdened down by life. He had a way of just hearing their reply to his greeting, noticing the tone, and addressing it right away. I am sure many of you have heard the saying, "you can tell a lot about someone just by looking into their eyes." Well, my dad can tell a lot about someone just by hearing their voice and tone! Many of us can make a difference in someone's life if we are willing to notice the signs they are giving out. Just like Dad could hear stress or hurt in their tone and begin to encourage someone, we can learn to do the same. People are more important than getting things done and marking things off our to-do lists.

That is another thing that sets Dad apart from so many other people. He did not allow his labeled disability to keep him from trying to help or aid someone. I remember when I was about 8 or 9 years old, we were on our way to church in Adrian, Missouri (a town eight miles from our farm). As soon as we turned off the highway, Dad said, "I smell something burning; I wonder what it is and where it is at." Mom kept driving towards the church, and the smell got stronger. We were about to turn down another street, where the church was, when a man ran out in the middle of the street, flailing his arms and hollering something. Mom stopped the van and asked the man what was going on. He said a house was on fire, and he thought his mom was still in there!

We looked over to the left of us and saw smoke billowing up, pouring out of a house just behind the one to our left. Dad hollered at Mom to get him right in front of the house and that he would go in and save her. I am telling you Mom and us girls were telling him he was crazy, that he would not be able to see anything, and that he was being ridiculous. We begged him to wait until the fire department arrived, but Dad would not listen! (They do say no one is more stubborn than Missouri stubborn.)

He jumped out of the van while the van was still slightly moving and headed toward the house on fire. He entered the house on his hands and knees and continued into the house, where he vanished for what seemed like forever. Mom and all of us girls were screaming, hollering, and praying because it felt like hours had transpired. The fire department finally arrived, and they ran in and helped Dad back outside. No one was inside the house, and we never saw the man we had seen outside flailing his arms again. The firefighters told Dad that he should never have done that, but Dad told them he was not about to have someone die if he could be of assistance.

When he returned to the van, I asked Dad why he did not just wait for the firefighters trained for those things. I asked why he felt he could find her better than the firefighters. I truly was not prepared for his answer. It impacted me even to today: "I have learned to use my ears, nose, hands, and feet to be my eyes for so long that I think I could have found her faster than someone who normally uses their eyes only."

You see, too many people discount any and everyone that is labeled with a disability. They do not want to give them a chance to try or showcase what they can do. If we would stop looking at the disabilities and see their abilities, then how much better would our world be? Suppose people would be more willing to take the time to help those with disabilities develop what they are exceptional in. If that were the case, we could learn much more from each other. Also, I feel it would make us all more well-rounded individuals.

See the ability and not the disability.

Dad-isms and replies...

"Dad, what time is it?"
"It is exactly half an hour from 30 minutes ago."

Chapter Seven
Hear It. Speak It. Receive It.
See It.

I never understood why I grew up so differently from my peers. When I was younger, I felt I was short-changed. I felt I did not get to have all the fun and do all the things that everyone else could engage in. It is amazing that as you grow older, you begin to see and learn what is truly valuable and important in life. In time, I discovered that everything I thought was vital to have as a kid was not really that important. Maturing helps us to learn that love, trust, a good work ethic, and family are so much more valuable and desired than the latest toy or gadget.

For instance, you learn that having a solid relationship with Jesus is the most important thing. As you develop your relationship with Jesus, He puts wisdom in your path, and you intersect the why and how. The Lord has shown me much about how He used what I thought was a dumpy, crappy, poor upbringing to teach me the skills needed for His plan for my life. Before knowing the Lord personally, I would never have desired or agreed to become a Pastor's wife, let alone to become a minister myself. I would never have understood what vision is at all. Without coming to know Jesus and being exposed to all I experienced in what I thought was a poor life, I would never have trusted God at His Word without seeing it.

Do you know that saying, "I will believe it when I see it!"? That statement screams a lack of faith. Hebrews 11:1 says, "Now faith is the substance of things hoped for the evidence of things NOT SEEN" (emphasis added). So, if we say we must see it before we believe it, we are not walking in faith. Faith is what pleases God; believing what God says before you can see it. The Word tells us in Hebrews 11:6 that without faith, it is impossible to please God. Even in the natural, do you know when I believed my dad? When Dad said it, that is when I believed it. Then I saw it come to pass. **Hear it; speak it; receive it; see it.**

You see, what I have learned through all of this is to approach things the way God intends for us to approach them. God's Word says in Romans 10:17, "So then faith comes by hearing, and hearing by the word of God." Our *hearing* is where it starts. Remember all the stories of my dad? Over and over, I witnessed how Dad had to develop and fine-tune his hearing to truly thrive in this world. He leaned on his hearing more than any other sense. I would witness how he could hear something long before we could hear it and, for sure, before we could see it.

For example, when he would turn and say, "someone just turned down the road and is coming." That corner was at least a quarter of a mile away from the edge of our property.

He would hear them coming, say they were coming, and then we would see them coming. Another example was when a cow or horse was distressed, he could hear them from afar. He could hear them coming and discern that they were making a sound of distress that was not their typical sound. He would tell us that we needed to go down and find the one in distress. We would search until we found the one that he heard specifically.

He could also tell what was wrong with a vehicle by the different sounds it was making. He would say what he thought it was. Then Dad would feel around under the car's hood until he found the part he knew was making the sound and then change it if he could. **Hear it; speak it; receive it; see it.**

We often base everything in our lives on what we see or feel at the moment. And, I think that too often, whether we can see it or not (with our natural eyes) determines our perspective on the situation. A great example of this is the account in the Bible of Elisha and his servant. In 2 Kings 6:17, Elisha prayed to the Lord to open the eyes of the servant, and the Lord opened his eyes. He was able to see the large host of the army that was there. The servant was freaking out because the servant was relying on his natural eyes. He did not see any of that until the Lord opened his spiritual eyes to see what was happening. Elisha was not responding in distress and worry. He was able *to see* what the Lord had planned.

Just trusting only in what we see or feel will steer us wrong in this life. We are to **hear** the Word of the Lord, **speak** the Word of the Lord, **<u>receive</u>** the Word of the Lord, and then we shall <u>**see**</u> the Word of the Lord. Second Corinthians 5:7 tells us that ***we walk by faith, not sight.*** Please take a moment with me as we apply this to some natural things to aid in understanding.

Whether you are a parent or not, we have all *been children*, so I believe you can easily follow and even identify with this analogy. We raised two boys, who are now both grown. But when they were younger, there were times that we told our boys we were going on a trip. They (mostly Alex) would ask tons of questions about when we would get there, what it would look like there, where we would be going, etc. When we would tell them the details and talk about everything we could do when we got there, it was awesome to hear them repeat what we said with excitement. As we arrived at our destination and they could finally see the exact things we described to them before the trip, their reactions were precious. They would exclaim, "It is just like you said it would be," or "it is just as I imagined by how you talked about it!" There were times when how we described something or somewhere paled in comparison to the real thing—the full revealing was better than they could even imagine!

God asks us to believe Him at His Word, not believe it when we see it. For instance, He gave us the best possible description that our finite minds can handle in Revelation when He talks about Heaven and its grandeur. I have an amazing picture in my mind of what it will be like, but I know it is nowhere near what it will be when I actually get there. I can picture the streets made of gold, the crystal river, the gates of pearl, and the amazing display of jewels there. I can envision the immense light coming from Jesus that will radiate all over. I could go on and on with what I envision when I read about it all in the book of Revelation. And one could think about the various artists who have portrayed Heaven or the angels with beautiful expressions on canvas, in books or films. But the truth remains, they only go by what they can fathom as it is in their mind's eye. There have been multiple accounts of believers visiting Heaven, whether in a vision, dream, or encounter. But time after time, even they have difficulty putting everything they have seen into words. Because we must walk by faith, not sight, even the best descriptions will pale compared to the real thing—the full revealing will always be better! Better than any of us can even imagine!

Do not get me wrong, I greatly enjoy having great eyesight and seeing the details and colors of all the wonderful things. But I feel that too many people have relied on their physical sight to guide their spiritual walk and life. I was raised by a man who trusted his hearing to guide him first. He did that not only in the natural but in the spiritual.

Dad wants everyone to know about Jesus. He wants everyone to believe God's Word. He talks about God's Word all the time, wonders what God meant when He said a thing, and discusses what God said often. There were countless times I heard Dad ask the Lord for guidance in a situation on the farm. He depended on God to get him through each day. He relied on God's Word and trusted in the Lord to bring to his remembrance the Word. Dad could not just look up the verse or "google it." He would have to remember what He had already heard repeatedly from the audio version of the Bible. Dad listened to that daily, so he has it in his memory to draw from. If he wanted specifics, Dad would ask us girls (mostly Chris or me) or Mom to look up the scripture concerning what he was wondering about. I see now that because he could not search it, he had me search it—which got me more in the Word. I often remember spending an hour or so looking up various scriptures and passages that Dad wanted to learn or hear more about.

As a child growing up hearing the Word constantly through the audio-book, I tried to tune it out because it played all the time. Dad had his audio-book player going all the time, especially inside the house. Dad read other books occasionally, but he loved hearing the Word of the Lord and getting it into his heart and mind. It really should be no different for us in that manner. We are to hear the Word and hear the Word and then hear it again. Truly can you ever hear the Word too much? The Bible tells us in Psalm 119:11, *"Your word I have treasured and stored in my heart, that I may not sin against you"* (AMP). How do we hide God's Word in our hearts? By hearing it over and over again. Then we speak it over and over again. And we choose to receive what it says **as truth and life**. The more we hear it and speak it (believing what it says), the more it remains within us.

God has always had a desire, a design, and a plan for everyone on Earth. The Lord says, *"For I know the plans and thoughts that I have for you, says the Lord, plans for peace and well-being and not for disaster, to give you a future and a hope"* (Jeremiah 29:11 AMP). God desires you to fulfill the plan He has laid out for you. The Word says in Psalm 37, *"The Lord directs the steps of the godly. He delights in every detail of their lives"* (v. 23 NLT). Think about this: If God knows the number of hairs on our head (and he does), you can trust that He is a personal God. I am so thankful that God knows how to take something we think is no good or disastrous and make it work for our good. Isaiah tells us,

To all who mourn in Israel, he will give a crown of beauty for ashes, a joyous blessing instead of mourning, festive praise instead of despair. (Isaiah 61:3 NLT)

It was never easy to have to describe things in extreme detail so that Dad could figure out what something was. It was inconvenient, through the eyes of a child, to look up scriptures because Dad could not see to read the words on the page for himself. It was not fun repeating myself (over and over) when explaining a math problem to Dad because I needed help understanding how to work something out. But God! God used all those things to train me! I now utilize all those skills to become a better minister, teacher, mother, friend, daughter, and wife. It is amazing what all God can do!

I want to encourage you to transition your mindset from using your natural eyes to guide you. Begin to develop your other senses to create a well-rounded person—that will draw those super abilities drawn out of you. I venture to say that part of learning God's wisdom is learning how to allow yourself *to let God train* you in developing all your senses to work for your good.

Revisiting my thoughts from earlier chapters, when I was younger, I wanted to get into my dad's mind, see how he saw, and experience things as he did. I wanted to see how he was able to accomplish what he did. I wanted to do things exactly like he did. I tried to get into the mind of my dad. I wanted to smell like him. I yearned to hear as he did. I desired to develop all my senses to the fullest possible and be able to use them to navigate my world. I did not know it then, but that innate desire is exactly how it should be now as I live for Christ! *"Let this mind be in you which was also in Christ Jesus"* (Philippians 2:5 NKJV).

As Jesus walked this earth, he would only say what his Father said. He would only do what the Father had him do. He stayed completely in touch with the Father, who knew how to use all available to Him. Jesus listened so intently to what his Father said. Then he would say what his Father said. That is how He then saw the desired outcome of what He proclaimed.

Growing up, my dad always amazed me with how he did things. As I matured, I began to deeply appreciate what I learned from him. But my amazement at Dad pales in comparison to how God amazes me. Little did I know that all those years growing up attempting to figure out Dad's ways, God was preparing me for the true mind of Christ and helping me begin to see things His way. He has been training me to take the visions and dreams He has given me and wait for them to fully manifest into the natural realm, where I will see them with my natural eyes. He is teaching me to **hear** His Word, **speak** His Word, **receive** His Word, and then **see** His Word.

Dad-isms and enjoying life...

Dad enjoys life and enjoys "sampling" good food! I would often fix Dad's plate full of a variety of foods, and when I came to throw away his plate, I would ask if he wanted anything else. He always said, "Boy, that was just a sample; I wouldn't mind another."

Dad-isms and having fun...

"Dad, should I throw these rotten tomatoes over the fence to the cows?"

"Absolutely not; we don't waste good tomatoes. Those are the perfect tomatoes for a tomato fight!" (Which was said as he rushed to grab them and throw them at anyone around!)

Chapter Eight
Catch the Vision:
Made to See

No one can choose who their parents are, where they are born, how they are raised, or even people's treatment of them. We can, however, allow God to take all of these things and mold us into what He has already planned for us!

As you may have figured out by now, all of these enduring, endearing life stories (and those yet to be published, including more of what I fondly call "Dad-isms") tie in together to the plan of God—not only in my life but also in *yours*.

God will take all the good, bad, and ugly of our lives and fashion it into a beautiful tapestry of His redeeming grace for others to see. Our life is to display and demonstrate God's goodness; we are a visual exhibition of His Kingdom and His Glory.

In these final pages, I'd like to identify and spotlight the lives of others (real people) who heard the Word of the Lord, **caught the vision** of the Lord, and were **made to see** the hand, glory, and provision of God.

First, let us look at Noah. Noah was a family man. One day, God spoke to Noah and gave him specific instructions on building the ark that would save his family. He told him that there would be water that would come and there would be destruction upon the earth. (This is in Genesis chapter 6.) The thing is, this was something never witnessed before by anyone… ever! The book of Hebrews states,

> It was by faith that Noah built a large boat to save his family from the flood. He obeyed God, who warned him about things that had never happened before. By his faith, Noah condemned the rest of the world, and he received the righteousness that comes by faith. (Hebrews 11:7 NLT)

Noah trusted what God had said and continued to trust his word until he could see the Word come to pass. He was able to **catch the vision** and was **made to see** the salvation of the Lord.

Next, let us look at Abraham. In Genesis chapter 12, the Lord told Abraham (who was called *Abram* then) to leave his native land, his father's family, and relatives and go to the land where He would show him. He did not know where he was going but trusted the word he had heard from the Lord. He set out to journey to see that land. In Hebrews 11, often called *the great faith chapter*, the Lord credits Abraham's faithfulness as righteousness because he walked by faith and journeyed to that land that the Lord said He would show him. Abraham went from **hearing** the Word **to seeing** the Word with his natural eyes. He was able to **catch the vision** and was **made to see** the faithfulness of the Lord.

Then, there is Joseph! Joseph's account in the Word is a powerful example of a man who chose to **catch the vision**. When he was young, the Lord gave Joseph dreams concerning his favor and position of authority over his brothers and family. These dreams given to Joseph were given to him by the Lord. **He held onto them until they came into sight**. His brothers did not believe him, and even his father did not believe him. But he held onto what the Lord had given him. He trusted in the Lord and kept his faith in the Lord—**and he saw the fulfillment of this dream come into sight**.

Joseph's account is a great testament to the faithfulness of God and His Word. The power of vision and dreams, given to one by God, makes them worth seeing and holding onto. Joseph was able to **catch the vision** (holding fast to it by faith) and was **made to see** the provision and deliverance of the Lord.

Another great example is John and the book of Revelation. This is where we can find ourselves in the catching-the-vision process. The book of Revelation has not yet been fully fulfilled (seen in the earth), but it will be. We know that all God's promises are Yes and Amen. Countless numbers of prophecies written in the Word of God have already been fully fulfilled and have come to pass. There are still many prophesies that have not been fulfilled but will be one day.

John had to write down all that God had shown him and write it down in detail as God told him. We could go into great detail regarding the visions, dreams, and descriptions so richly recorded in Revelation. Still, we will refrain from that right now and say that the short version of it is, John had to **catch the vision** of what God said and record it for all the generations after him to have access to. He was **made to see** it through the experience the Lord gave him. And we will be made to see it one day when the prophecies are completely fulfilled!

Now let us tie this into how this can be helpful in our lives. Suppose someone has a dream, vision, or plan that they excitedly share with you. As they describe it to you in detail (perhaps with great passion in their voice as they share it), often one of the first responses out of our mouths is, "I can see it!" That is because of how they have described it in detail. Even though it is not physically in our natural realm of eyesight, we can envision it as they describe it. It is the same thing when it comes to things of God.

When we hear a Word from the Lord, we are to envision it personalized to us and claim it as ours because… it is for us! We then continually hold onto the Word by speaking it—over and over (because faith comes by hearing and hearing the Word of God)—to keep it *top of mind* (in the forefront of our minds and lives). We must keep it ever in our supernatural vision until it comes fully in sight in our natural eyes.

Just like Joseph's dreams became exactly as he dreamt them years later, saving his family and many other families; just like Noah's obedience to the Word of the Lord in building an ark preserved every created animal and his family as he held onto what he heard, worked according to God's vision and plan, and then saw the Lord's salvation; just like Abraham listened to God say go, and he followed the instructions of the Lord; and just like John's supernatural encounter with the Lord brought about such descriptive prophetic poetry of God's divine deep love for a people...

Just like these, **we can catch the vision and be made to see all God has in store for us.**

Throughout my own life, the Lord started giving me visions and dreams, beginning when I was incredibly young. Many would scare me because I never really understood what they meant. They were so vivid and in color that it was as if I was living it in a movie. I tried to share them with Dad and Mom, but they did not understand and always thought it was a silly old dream or nightmare.

Many nights I would wake up and have difficulty going back to sleep, trying to decipher what they meant or what I had done wrong to have these. There were even nights I was afraid to even close my eyes in the event I would have a dream. I started to dismiss them and attempted to shove them in the back of my mind or ask that they be removed from my memory completely, never to be remembered again.

There were even times that while I was awake in the night, I could see visions appear right before me that frightened me. Scenes in real motion and outlined figures; even wiping my eyes could not clear them away.

I did not understand, nor was I taught that it was alright to have things like that come into my mind and not understand them. It was all a learning process that the Lord had to teach me through others who understood visions and dreams. It was not until recently that the Lord revealed the meaning of one of those "scary" visions I had when I was around 8 or 9 years old.

The visions and dreams of the Lord never go away. He gives you them to hold onto for such a time that He has for them to unfold. **Trusting the Word of the Lord and holding on to the visions and dreams placed in front of you is vital for seeing their revealing**.

The Word of God has never failed me, and it never will. His Word is truth. It is Life and health to me. It is protection, safety, and strength. The Word spoken causes it to be heard, which causes faith to come. Faith pleases the Father. Faith in the Lord unlocks so much for everyone who lives and walks in Faith. Faith comes by hearing the Word of God.

We must allow the Lord to develop our hearing, for it is by hearing the anointed Word of God that we **catch the vision** and are **made to see,** first through the Word and then (at His revealing) with our natural eyes.

I want to encourage you that God has a vision He has already placed within you. Allow the Holy Spirit to heal your vision to **see what He sees** *for you*. Allow Him to supply each aspect of the vision for your life so that you can encounter the fullness of that vision. I encourage you to watch Him develop your spiritual sight so that when you hear His Word, you grab hold of it and speak it in agreement. Through this, you will gain knowledge and understanding of His Word. Your faith will grow because you have allowed your hearing to grab hold of His Word.

Learning to See Through Blinded Eyes

The Kingdom of God is far beyond just what our natural eyes behold. But our natural eyes will behold the Kingdom of God by hearing first, then faith, and then sight. The Word tells us that God's ways are higher than our ways. That sounds so simple, but we tend to want to complicate it. Tap into the Holy Spirit and allow him to heal the blind eyes of vision so that you may begin to see all He has in store for you. The book of Habakkuk tells us, *"Write the vision and make it plain on tablets, that he may run who reads it"* (Habakkuk 2:2 NKJV). Vision is an important aspect of walking with Christ. Write down what God has spoken or shown you in the spirit. Then speak it faithfully—over and over (because faith comes by hearing and hearing the Word of God)—and you will see it come to pass.

One final thing before we press pause on the stories and close this book...

When I asked Dad recently what he looked forward to seeing when he went home to heaven, his answer was nothing I expected. With tears in his eyes yet with a shimmer of joy, he stated, "To be able to sit at Jesus's feet. To give Him praise, honor, and glory for the things that he has done for us kids, especially me. You see, I have to answer to Him."

My heart melted at that statement. Here is a man who, for most of his life, had skewed eyesight and then deteriorating eyesight to a point where he can only see small sections of light, and that only occasionally. He does not want to see what his mother's face looks like. He does not want to see his wife's face and figure. He does not want to see the crystal river and the streets of gold. He does not want to see every detail in color. He does not even want to ask why he wasn't healed and could see fully while here on the earth.

He wants to sit at the feet of the one who died for him. He wants to praise Jesus for everything he has done for him. As a little girl, I wanted to imitate my dad in every way possible. To let you in on something… I still do! I want to have such a love for Jesus, the Word of the Lord, the creator God, the guiding Holy Spirit that I am not asking the *why not's* or the *what for's* but just to sit at His feet and give him praise and glory for all He has done.

The voice of God said, (referring to Jesus, recorded in Luke 9:35 NKJV) "This is My beloved Son. Hear Him!"

I want to hear Him.

In my husband's words (Pastor Jason Houston), **"Perfect hearing always produces seeing."** I want to allow the Lord to develop my every sense so that all are so keen that He can use me for his glory with the foreknowledge of things as needed to advance His kingdom.

One day, just as he desires to, my dad will hear God speak to him,

Well done, my good and faithful servant. You have been faithful in handling this small amount, so now I will give you many more responsibilities. Let's celebrate together. (Matthew 25: 21 NLT)

Dad will be able to sit at the feet of Jesus and give him praise, honor, and glory for all He has done. But he will also see every detail of every person that has gone on before him. Dad will see every shade of every color. He will experience the streets of gold that will shimmer fully in his eyes. He will be able to look off in the distance and see with complete clarity all of the glory of Heaven. The trees, the angels, the saints, the throne of God, the King of Glory, and so much more. Every detail described to us in the book of Revelation… Dad will see. He will spend the rest of eternity seeing what he envisioned as he heard the Word spoken. *What an astounding thought!*

Even more amazing perhaps is that not only do I have the assurance that *Dad* will experience it (because of his choice to receive Christ as Savior), but when my day comes to enter my eternal home, *I will also.* Because of my own choice to receive Christ as my Savior, I will also see and encounter all the glory of Heaven! I will have the joy to witness my dad seeing in all fullness for eternity! No doubt, he and I will sit and discuss the details of it all as we compare and experience it all together. **Will you join us?**

The Word says that even while we were yet in sin, Christ died for us. He came so that none would perish but that all would have eternal life. I pray you've been inspired by the stories in this book, but most of all, I pray that you've seen faith, hope, and the love of God present in them all. I pray it has inspired you to yield your life to the Father and learn to see through **Daddy's Eyes.**

Notes

1   Tim O'Neil, "A Look Back: The Relentless, Withering Heat Wave of 1936 Killed 479 in St. Louis," STLtoday.com (St. Louis Post-Dispatch, July 30, 2022), https://www.stltoday.com/news/archives/a-look-back-the-relentless-withering-heat-wave-of-1936-killed-479-in-st-louis/article_3821b7be-14c4-5fef-b0c9-bc383d50aafd.html (accessed March 7, 2023).

2   Pearson, Stephen. "What Happened in 1936 Including Significant Events, Key Technology," The People History. https://www.thepeoplehistory.com/1936.html (accessed March 7, 2023).

3   III, Joe Hummel. "1936 Trivia, History and Fun Facts - Pop Culture: History: Facts: Trivia." Pop Culture | History | Facts | Trivia, November 22, 2021. https://popculturemadness.com/PCM/1936/1936-trivia-history-and-fun-facts/ (accessed March 7, 2023).

4   Author's note: The story is shared with no disrespect intended. The "nuthouse" is what the mid-west rural culture of the era commonly called mental institutions. Patients with tuberculosis, nervous breakdowns, or other diseases that caused mental instability were often sent there to live because medical science had no other treatment to offer. Modern culture has grown in knowledge and treatment options, which has changed our treatment, care, as well as our vocabulary. Still, it was not uncommon during that era for it to be called either "the nuthouse" or "the insane asylum." So without any intended malice toward the patients, further details were intentionally omitted so that the humor of what was their admittedly funny first date story could be included, while being sensitive to others in the story.

Meet the Author

Rachel Houston is the co-founder of Houston Faith Ministries and co-host/co-pastor of the WORD for Life Movement, a daily teaching and ministry broadcast streaming live on multiple social media platforms.

Pastor Rachel has faithfully served the church alongside her husband in team ministry for over twenty years (at the time of publishing this book). They have pastored churches in Missouri, Arkansas, New Mexico, Tennessee, and Texas. Her gracious and diligent walk of faith has earned her regard as a prophet, anointed preacher, gifted musician and psalmist, and loving pastor. With a special elegance and spirit of excellence, she has served in almost every capacity in the church while at the same time, she gracefully fulfills the roles of a dedicated school teacher, wife, and mother.

Rachel Houston has a unique appreciation for life and ministry. She is the daughter of Leroy Welch, originally from Butler, Missouri, and raised on a rural century farm outside of Passaic, Missouri. Rachel attended school in Butler and continued by studying Music and Vocal Instruction and Education at the College of the Ozarks. She also graduated with a degree in Elementary Education from the University of New Mexico and holds a Master's Degree in Special Education from the University of Arkansas.

Rachel has taken full advantage of the insight, knowledge, and revelation gained from years working with family members and friends with various impairments and challenges. This experience has helped her become a highly effective classroom teacher to students of all ages throughout her tenure in general education and special education.

In this, her first published book, Rachel tells the story of God's great faithfulness as seen in the life of her Dad as he recalls growing up with five other siblings with visual impairments. This book recounts the triumph of this family as they refused to allow their impairment and challenges to become a disability. It is the story of God's faithfulness and the believer's victory. You will be inspired to trust the hand of God at work in your life as you allow love to heal, hope to rise, and faith to yield true sight!

For more information regarding the ministry of Rachel Houston, please visit: http://houstonfaithministries.com